Editor
Kim Fields

Editorial Project Manager
Mara Ellen Guckian

Editor-in-Chief
Sharon Coan, M.S. Ed.

Illustrator
Kelly McMahon

Cover Artist
Brenda DiAntonis

Art Manager
Kevin Barnes

Art Director
CJae Froshay

Imaging
James Edward Grace
Richard E. Easley

Product Manager
Phil Garcia

Publisher
Mary D. Smith, M.S. Ed.

Author

Shirley B. Spriegel M.S. Ed.

Teacher Created Resources, Inc.
6421 Industry Way
Westminster, CA 92683
www.teachercreated.com

ISBN-0-7439-3380-X

©2004 Teacher Created Resources, Inc.

Reprinted, 2005

Made in U.S.A.

Table of Contents

Table of Contents *(cont.)*

Introduction

Here it is! The research has been done for you! Designed for the busy teacher, this is a practical guide to teaching the alphabetic principle through a multi-sensory, thematic approach. *Getting Ready to Read* incorporates activities and patterns for all areas of the curriculum in one handy guide. This book will help you design plans for beginning readers that incorporate new and time-tested strategies for learning the letters of the alphabet.

Teachers can help students with phonemic awareness and phonics by providing a program rich in language activities. In order to decode—figure out the words—students must develop a knowledge of letters. Students will become familiar with the alphabetic principle while they are listening to stories, doing art activities, trying different foods, learning about science, making crafts, and singing songs connected to the letter or digraph they are working on each day. We recognize that students have different learning styles, or combinations of styles. Think about the ways your students learn. According to Howard Gardner, the different learning styles include the following:

- Verbal/Linguistic Learners
- Logical/Mathematical Learners
- Visual/Spatial Learners
- Bodily/Kinesthetic Learners

- Musical Learners
- Interpersonal Learners
- Intrapersonal Learners
- Naturalist Learners

When learning is fun children learn new material more easily and remember it longer. There's something for everyone in this book. After introducing the first or second letter, students will look forward to the sequence of activities with the security of a familiar routine.

Overview

Reading Component

The goal of this book is to use the suggested books and activities to teach and reinforce the most often used sounds for the twenty-six letters of the alphabet and four digraphs (two letters that make one sound). Students are introduced to the letter with a "Special Picture." The letter, the letter sound, and the "Special Picture" are reinforced consistently with language arts and other curriculum activities. In order to decode (figure out the words) students must develop knowledge of letters and sounds, the building blocks of words. This is accomplished in several ways: letter recognition, phonemic awareness (oral manipulation of sounds), phonics (the written transcription of sounds using letters), learning sight words, syllabication, rhyming, and recognition of word patterns.

A child is said to be phonemically aware when he or she can identify individual sounds (phonemes) in oral language. There are five levels of phonemic awareness, listed from the easiest to the most difficult.

- rhyming—determining if two or more words rhyme; naming rhyming words
- noting similarities and differences in beginning, middle, and ending sounds
- blending—listening to a series of sounds (phonemes), connecting them, and identifying the word they make /c/ /a/ /t/ = cat
- segmenting words into phonemes, *cat* = /c/ /a/ /t/
- manipulating phonemes to create new words, *cat—can, bag—bat—hat*

Overview *(cont.)*

Reading Component *(cont.)*

The importance of reading to children cannot be overestimated. Every new story holds the possibility of new words and strengthens the students' understanding of the way language works.

Reading to children . . .

- aids oral language development

- stimulates curiosity about the world

- develops familiarity with written text (concepts of print)

- increases comprehension

- increases vocabulary

- can serve as a leaping-off point for discussions by asking *who, what, when, where, why,* and *how* questions. These discussions aid in the development of higher-order, critical thinking skills.

- familiarizes them with left to right orientation

Handwriting Component

Printing practice promotes letter knowledge and increases phonic awareness. Students should be encouraged to write letters, parts of words, and words as soon as they know some of the letters of the alphabet. Teaching letter formation from the beginning, in conjunction with letter identification, reinforces phonics with tactile reinforcement. Consistent practice is very important. There is a direct relationship between writing correctly and reading.

Reinforcement Activities

The activities included for each letter and digraph cover most curriculum areas. The activities are fun and include movement, hands-on involvement, and practice in a variety of skill areas. Incorporating some or all of these activities will allow the new letters and sounds to be focused on throughout the day.

Food and snack suggestions are also given for each letter or digraph. (**Safety alert:** Always check student allergy lists before serving new snacks). Add other items popular with your students.

Overview *(cont.)*

Special Pictures

The objective for teaching the letters using the "Special Pictures" is for the students to: *See* the letter with the object. *Recall* the object. *Remember* the beginning sound. The "Special Pictures" chosen for this book are shown below.

Aa—apple   Bb—ball   Cc—cat   Dd—dog   Ee—elephant

Ff—fish   Gg—girl   Hh—hat   Ii—insect   Jj—jar

Kk—kite   Ll—lion   Mm—mouse   Nn—nest   Oo—octopus

Pp—pig   Qq—queen   Rr—rabbit   Ss—sun   Tt—turtle

Uu—umbrella   Vv—valentine   Ww—watermelon   Xx—box   Yy—yarn

Zz—zebra   Ch—chick   Sh—ship   Th—thumb   Wh—whale

How to Use This Book

Set the Stage

It is important that each lesson begin with great enthusiasm. Show an object or picture of something connected with the book you are reading. The item should begin with the letter and the correct letter sound. For instance, a fish in a bowl for the letter **Ff**, or a calendar of dog pictures for the letter **Dd**, or a toy elephant for the letter **Ee**. Related books are listed that are appropriate for young children. Read during the school day to reinforce the beginning letter sound and the topics you are discussing. Give this recommended list to the school librarian in advance to borrow, or keep these books in your own collection. (**Suggestion:** Keep all the materials, books, and patterns in a storage box labeled with a letter of the alphabet. Then, as you find or develop these materials, you can file them together for easy access.)

Introduce the Literature

Show the cover of the book you have chosen and read the title. Point out the letter you are teaching. Encourage predictions about what might happen in the book. For some books, it is a good idea to do a picture walk at this time to help implant the language or vocabulary the students will be hearing in the story. Simply go through the book with students, sharing each illustrated page. Read the literature. Allow time for discussion of the book and discuss the predictions made before reading. Reintroduce the letter by putting the letter at the top of a chart and brainstorming a list of words beginning with it. List the words under the letter while asking students to pay attention to the beginning letter. Include any names of students that begin with the letter. Introduce the three special words that will become sight words. These words are highlighted at the top of the introductory page for each letter or digraph. Put the three sight words on cards and arrange them in an alphabetical list on the wall. Encourage students to use the words on the wall when they are writing. (**Management Tip:** If a student says a word that is inconsistent with the sound or letter you are teaching, for instance, "kitten" for the letter **Cc**, agree that the sound is correct, but tell students that the word is not spelled that way. Explain that it starts with another letter beginning with a similar sound. Do not put it on your list.)

Construct Meaning

Ask students to share something they know or have experienced connected with the featured letter or with the book they have just heard. Frequent use of word webs helps children to become accustomed to activating and articulating prior knowledge. Foods and snack possibilities beginning with the letter are listed for you. Tasting and smelling foods and cooking projects add further associations connected to the letter. Teachers should always be aware of food allergies.

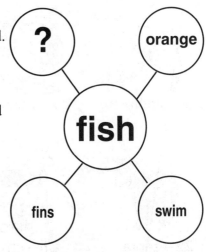

Review the Skill Lesson

Discuss the magic picture and special words. Review the list of brainstormed words on a regular basis. Continue to add any other words students may think of to the list.

How to Use this Book (cont.)

Handwriting

Demonstrate correct letter formation. Practice writing the uppercase and lowercase letters on the worksheets provided. If appropriate, an additional worksheet is provided to practice writing the three special words that begin with the letter you are working on and to write a sentence. Encourage students to use as many words that are phonetically consistent with the sounds you are teaching as possible. (A <u>big</u> <u>bug</u> <u>bit</u> <u>Bob</u>.)

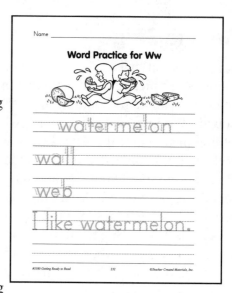

Reinforcement Activities

Reinforce the sound of the letter by using some of the suggested science, art, songs, and other activities throughout the day. Keep mentioning that you are doing the activity because of the beginning sound of the letter. Arts, crafts, and music activities are very important for the growth of literacy skills in young children. They not only include opportunities for active learning, but also appeal to tactile, kinesthetic, and musical learners. Art work and projects on the classroom walls or sent to the child's home will provide opportunities for the child to discuss the picture and the letter. The use of arts and crafts helps children build literacy skills in a fun, hands-on, relaxed environment. In addition, suggestions are given to help plan activities that allow for movement in and outside of the classroom.

Science suggestions are given to appeal to the natural curiosity of young children. The students will learn about the constancy of scientific principles, such as animal habitats, that roots grow down and stems grow up, and that water can freeze or thaw depending on the temperature. All of these "grand" ideas help children feel more secure in a sometimes uncertain world.

In today's busy classroom, teaching science with literacy makes sense. The busy teacher can incorporate the science curriculum right into language arts instruction. Children will recall both science and letter knowledge more easily because they have been taught thematically, and the teacher achieves a balance between teaching skills and nonfiction knowledge.

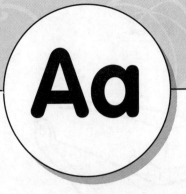

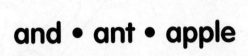

Story Books

Alexander and the Terrible, Horrible, No-Good, Very Bad Day by Judith Viorst

Alligator Baby by Robert Munsch

Alligators All Around: An Alphabet Book by Maurice Sendak

And to Think That I Saw It on Mulberry Street by Dr. Seuss

Angela's Airplane by Robert Munsch

Anteater Named Arthur by Bernard Waber

Apples and Pumpkins by Anne Rockwell

Rainforest Animals by Paul Hess

Seasons of Arnold's Apple Tree by Gail Gibbons

There's an Alligator Under My Bed by Mercer Mayer

Foods/Snacks

- animal crackers
- apple juice
- apples
- applesauce
- apricots

Getting Started

1. Introduce the letter and the special picture. Read a book with the letter **A** in the title. Brainstorm a list of other words that begin with **Aa** and write the words on a chart. Include the names of any children in the class whose names begin with **A**. (**Note:** When introducing the students to any of the activities or worksheets connected to the letter, the emphasis should be on the connection to the letter and the letter sound.)

2. Discuss "Action" words. Dramatize the following words: *run, skip, tip-toe, walk, jump, jog,* and *hop.*

Language Arts for Aa

My Favorite Animal Book

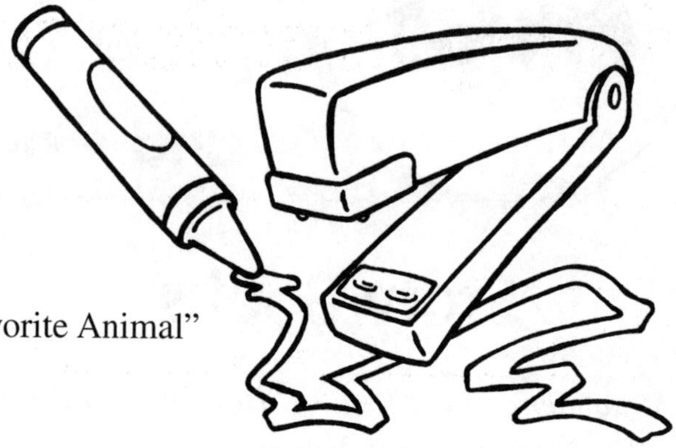

Materials

- enlarged and duplicated sheets (see below).
- crayons or markers
- staples and stapler
- cover for the class book with the title, "My Favorite Animal"

Procedure

1. Make a class book entitled, "My Favorite Animal." Have each child decide on an animal to draw and draw the animal, being careful not to draw over the writing. As an alternative, this is a good time to use technology to download an animal picture.

2. Write the name of the animal on the line. (If the child needs help with this, the word can be written on a small card for the child to copy.)

3. Stack the completed book pages together and add the cover. Staple the pages together.

4. As you go through the book with the children, have each child stand and read his or her page.

- -

Name

_____

_____

My favorite animal is _____.

- -

Name _____

Printing Practice for Aa

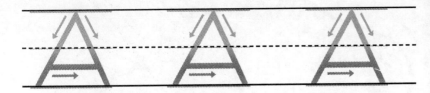

apple

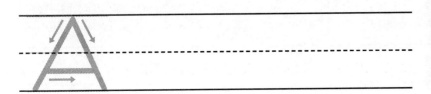

Word Practice for Aa

apple

and

ant

I have an apple.

12

Science Activities for Aa

Animal Classification Game

Make an animal classification game to practice classifying animals with backbones.

Materials

- old magazines or calendars
- 60" x 48" (150 cm x 120 cm) piece of fabric or butcher paper
- permanent marker

Preparation: Cut out pictures of animals from old magazines or calendars or download pictures from your computer. Draw lines to divide the fabric or paper into six blocks. In each block, write one of the following, "Animals Without Backbones," "Mammals," "Reptiles," "Birds," "Amphibians," or "Fish."

Procedure

1. Discuss the different characteristics of the six featured animal groups:

Animals Without Backbones	Mammals
Birds	Reptiles
Amphibians	Fish

   Mammals—hair or fur, warm bodies, feed milk to babies

   Birds—feathers, two legs, two wings, babies hatch from eggs

   Fish—live and breathe under water, have cold bodies, some have fins

   Reptiles—dry skin, scales, four short legs or none at all

   Amphibians—smooth wet skin, live on land and water, lay eggs

   Animals Without Backbones—insects, animals with shells

2. Have students spread the cloth out on the floor.

3. Direct students to look at each picture and decide which box it should go in.

4. Allow students to use this game independently. Put pictures in the correct box. Write the name of the correct group on the back of each picture before placing it in the independent center.

Ants on an Anthill

Discuss that ants are insects. Insects have three body parts, two antennae, six legs, and lay eggs. Ants work together and live in hills of dirt with many rooms.

Materials

- *Ant Cities* by Arthur Dorros
- 9" x 6" (23 cm x 15 cm) sheets of black paper (one per child)
- white pencils
- scissors
- glue
- brown paper

Preparation: Use a white pencil to trace three ovals, six strips for legs, and two shorter strips for antennae on each sheet of black paper. Draw a large anthill on the brown paper.

Procedure

1. Read a nonfiction book about ants, such as *Ant Cities*.

2. Give each child a black paper pattern sheet to cut out the body parts.

3. Have students glue the parts together and then glue the assembled ant on the anthill.

4. Discuss how students have cooperated to make an anthill, just like ants work together. Display the picture with the title, "Ants on an Anthill." Draw attention to each **Aa**.

Art Activities for Aa

Animal Masks

Materials

- paper plates (one per child)
- scissors
- string
- crayons or markers
- scraps of colored paper; straws for whiskers
- glue

Preparation: Cut two holes in each paper plate for eye holes.

Procedure

1. As a group, discuss possibilities for animal masks. Model the activity before asking students to begin making masks.
2. Have the students color the paper plate to look like an animal. Students might use gray for an elephant; orange and black stripes for a tiger; yellow and orange for a lion; etc.
3. Glue on ears cut from colored scrap paper.
4. While the children are coloring, poke holes in the sides of the paper plate and attach strings long enough to tie behind the student's head.
5. Play marching or circus music and have a parade.

Apple Wreaths

Materials

- paper plates (one per child)
- apple pattern (page 15)
- red, yellow, and green crayons or markers
- scissors
- glue
- string

Preparation: Cut a 5" (13 cm) circle out of the center of each paper plate. Punch a hole at the top of each plate for hanging. Duplicate the apple patterns twice for each child. (**Option:** Copy the apple patterns onto colored construction paper.)

Procedure

1. Color the apples red, yellow, or green (if not using colored patterns).
2. Cut out the apples.
3. Glue the apples around the edge of the paper plate. Tell students to paste the apples at the top, bottom, on each side, and then one in between each apple on the plate.
4. Attach string through the hole and hang up the finished wreath.

Apple Wreaths

Apple Patterns

Each student will need two copies of this page.

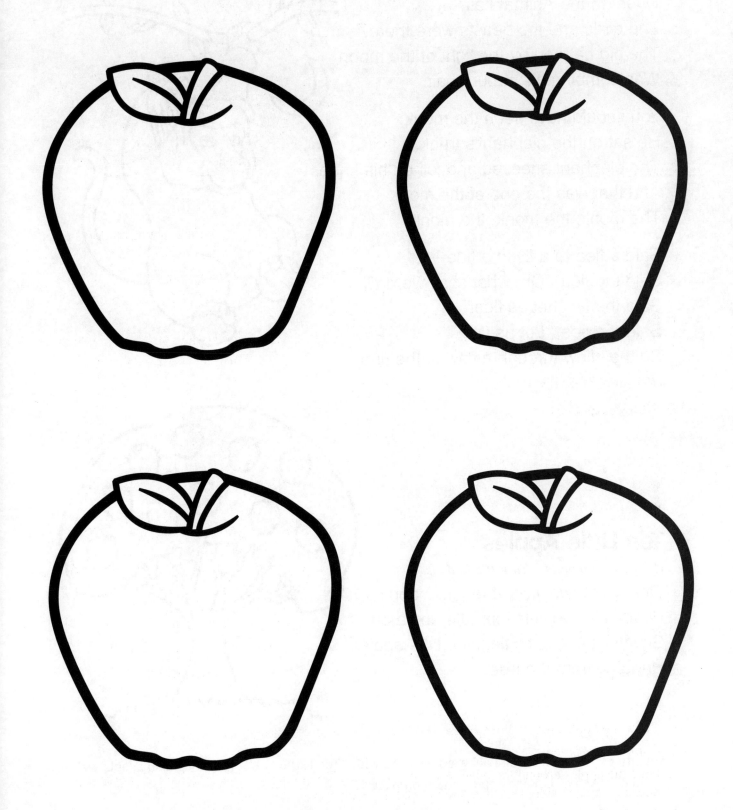

Songs and Fingerplays for Aa

The Animal Fair

(Traditional)

I went to the Animal Fair.
The birds and the beasts were there.
The big baboon by the light of the moon
Was combing his auburn hair.

You should have seen the monk.
He sat on the elephant's trunk.
The elephant sneezed and fell on his knees
And that was the end of the monk
The monk, the monk, the monk.

Said a flea to a fly in a flue—
Said the flea, "Oh, what shall we do?"
Said the fly, "Let us flee!"
Said the flea, "Let us fly!"
So they flew through a flaw in the flue.

(Repeat the first two verses.)

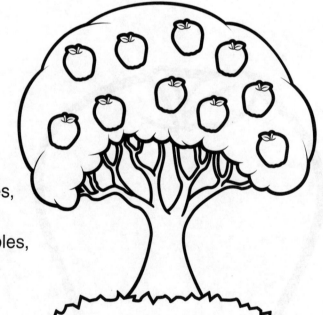

Ten Little Apples

(Sing to the tune of "Ten Little Indians.")
One, little, two little, three little apples,
Four little, five little, six little apples,
Seven little, eight little, nine little apples,
Hanging from the tree.

Variations: Sing the song backward, starting with "Ten Little. . . ." This song also adapts well to a feltboard story. Use the apple pattern on page 15.

Songs and Fingerplays for Aa *(cont.)*

Ants Go Marching

(Traditional)

The ants go marching one by one, hurrah, hurrah.

The ants go marching one by one, hurrah, hurrah.

The ants go marching one by one,

The little one stops to beat his drum,

And they all go marching down to the ground.

To get out of the rain, BOOM! BOOM! BOOM!

The ants go marching two by two, hurrah, hurrah.

The ants go marching two by two, hurrah, hurrah.

The ants go marching two by two,

The little one stops to tie his shoe,

And they all go marching down to the ground

To get out of the rain, BOOM! BOOM! BOOM!

The ants go marching three by three, hurrah, hurrah.

The ants go marching three by three, hurrah, hurrah.

The ants go marching three by three,

The little one stops to climb a tree,

And they all go marching down to the ground

To get out of the rain, BOOM! BOOM! BOOM!

The ants go marching four by four, hurrah, hurrah…

The little one stops to shut the door

The ants go marching five by five, hurrah, hurrah…

The little one stops to take a dive

The ants go marching six by six, hurrah, hurrah…

The little one stops to pick up sticks

The ants go marching seven by seven, hurrah, hurrah…

The little one stops to count to eleven

The ants go marching eight by eight, hurrah, hurrah…

The little one stops to shut the gate

The ants go marching nine by nine, hurrah, hurrah…

The little one stops to check the time

The ants go marching ten by ten, hurrah, hurrah…

The little one stops to say, "The end."

My Pocket Book for Aa

Aa

ant

1

apple

2

An ant is on an apple.

3

18

Bb

ball • bat • boy

Story Books

The Bear on the Bed by Ruth Miller

Ben's Trumpet by Rachel Isadora

Big Hungry Bear by Don & Audrey Wood

Blueberries for Sal by Robert McCloskey

Brown Bear, Brown Bear, What Do You See?
  by Bill Martin, Jr.

Bunny Trouble by Hans Wilhelm

Little Bear by Else Holmelund Minarik

Little Blue and Little Yellow by Leo Lionni

Monarch Butterfly by Gail Gibbons

The Story of Babar by Jean de Brunhoff

Foods/Snacks

- banana bread
- bananas
- biscuits
- blueberries
- bread
- broccoli
- butter

Getting Started

1. Introduce the letter and the special picture. Read a book with the letter **B** in the title. Brainstorm a list of other words that begin with a **Bb** and write the words on a chart. Include the names of any children in the class whose names begin with **B**. (**Note:** When introducing the students to any of the activities or worksheets connected to the letter, the emphasis should be on the connection to the letter and the letter sound.)

2. Bounce balls. You will need a ball (assorted sizes) for each child. Demonstrate bouncing and catching. Then individually bounce and catch balls. Bounce the ball again and have each student try to pass his or her leg over the ball as it bounces. Then bounce the ball to another child who will then bounce it back.

Language Arts for Bb

Bring-Your-Bear-to-School Day

Materials
- large cardboard box
- chart paper and marker
- note to parents
- large label for box

Preparation: Write a note to parents, requesting each child bring a stuffed bear to school on a specific day. Write "Box of Bears" on the large label.

Procedure
1. Each student holds up his or her bear and tells something about it (where he or she got it, a description of its size or color, what he or she does with it at home).
2. Write one sentence on chart paper for each student; then cut each child's sentence into a strip.
3. Place the bears around the room.
4. Read each sentence strip and place it by the appropriate bear.
5. Place the bears in the box labeled, "Box of Bears."

Book Fun

Materials
- *Brown Bear, Brown Bear, What Do You See?* by Bill Martin, Jr.
- sheets of white construction paper (one per child)
- colored paper
- scissors
- glue
- pencils
- crayons or markers
- chart paper and marker
- animal pictures or cutouts

Procedure
1. Read the book to students, pointing out the sequence of the book and how each animal sees an animal of a different color.
2. On chart paper, brainstorm a color and the animal possibilities for that color.
3. The student chooses a color and an animal, and writes/dictates a sentence on the bottom of the construction paper using the format of the book. (I see a _____ _____.)
4. Choose an animal picture or pattern and glue it above the sentence.
5. Finish the picture using crayons or markers.

Name _____

Printing Practice for Bb

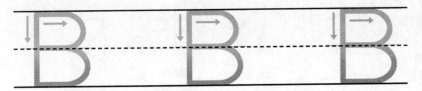

ball

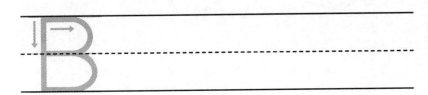

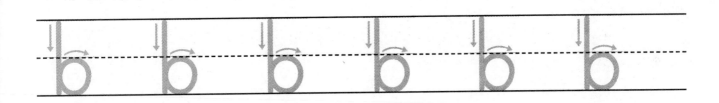

Word Practice for Bb

ball

bait

boy

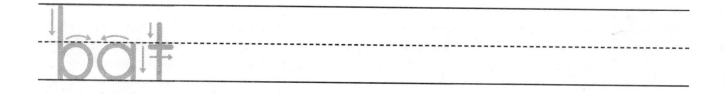

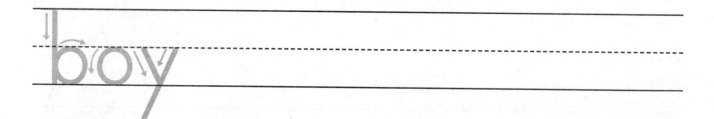

I have a ball.

Science Activities for Bb

Bees Build Honeycombs

Read a nonfiction book about bees. Make a honeycomb and place facts about bees on strips of paper inside the honeycomb.

Materials

- *The Honey Makers* by Gail Gibbons or
  The Bee by Sabrina Crewe
- toilet-paper tubes
- 10" x 12" x 5" (25 cm x 30 cm x 13 cm) cardboard box
- glue
- chart paper and marker
- scissors or papercutter (for teacher)

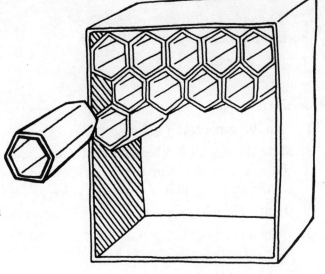

Procedure

1. Tell students to listen carefully for facts about bees and point out the honeycomb with six-sided holes while reading the book.

2. After reading the book, record facts about bees on the chart paper. Cut them apart into sentence strips.

3. Make a honeycomb by folding toilet-paper tubes in half and then in thirds. Open them up and pinch along the folds to make a hexagon. Put glue along one side length, place the tube in the box with the hole side out, and repeat the process until all the hexagons are put together forming a honeycomb.

4. Starting at the short side, roll up the fact strips and put them into the holes when the glue is dry.

5. Play a game by taking the strips out and having students read them.

Butterfly Life Cycle

Read a nonfiction book about the life cycle of butterflies. Show the stages of a butterfly's life on a circle.

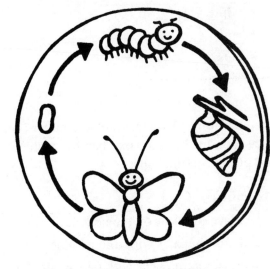

Materials

- *From Caterpillar to Butterfly* by Deborah Heiligman or *Becoming Butterflies* by Anne Rockwell
- paper plates (one per child)
- crayons or markers

Procedure

1. Read a book about butterflies.

2. Draw a caterpillar at the top of the plate, a chrysalis on the right side, a butterfly at the bottom, and an egg on the left side.

3. Draw a line with an arrow coming from each picture to show the sequence of the stages.

4. Display with butterflies such as the ones suggested in "Butterflies" (page 24).

Art Activities for Bb

Butterflies

Materials

- white paper towels (one per child)
- clothespins, with round tops (one per child)
- food coloring, diluted with water
- cotton swabs
- chenille sticks (one per child)
- newspaper
- markers

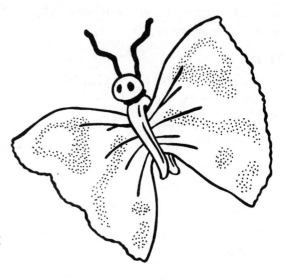

Procedure

1. Fold the paper towel in half.
2. Make dots of food coloring on the paper towel using cotton swabs. Open up the paper towel and place it on newspaper until it is completely dry.

   (**Hint:** Folding the paper towels will result in a symmetrical butterfly.)
3. Wrap a chenille stick around the "neck" of the clothespin to form antennae. Draw dots on the "head" for the eyes.
4. Gather the paper towel through the center and push into the clothespin.
5. Wave the completed butterfly in the air while singing "Butterfly Song" (see page 26).

Fuzzy Bears

Materials

- bear pattern (page 25)
- sheets of brown paper or brown paper bags (one per child)
- white glue
- small cups
- oats
- paintbrushes
- newspaper

Preparation: Duplicate the bear pattern onto brown paper, or trace it onto a brown paper bag for each child. Dilute the glue and place it in the cups.

Procedure

1. Place the bear on the newspaper.
2. Paint the bear with diluted glue.
3. Sprinkle the bear with oats while the glue is still wet.
4. Display the bears with the title, "Fuzzy, Wuzzy Bears," after they are dry.
5. Sing the song, "Fuzzy Wuzzy Was a Bear" (see page 26).

Fuzzy Bears

Bear Pattern

Trace this pattern onto brown paper or a brown paper bag for each student.

Songs and Fingerplays for Bb

Butterfly Song

(Sing to the tune of "Mary Had a Little Lamb.")
Flying, flying in the sky
In the sky, in the sky,
See the pretty butterfly,
Flying in the sky.

Fuzzy Wuzzy Was a Bear

(Traditional)
Fuzzy Wuzzy was a bear.
Fuzzy Wuzzy had no hair.
Fuzzy Wuzzy wasn't fuzzy.
Was he?

Baby Bumblebee

(Traditional)
I'm bringing home a baby bumblebee,
(Cup hands.)
Won't my Mommy be so proud of me.
I'm bringing home a baby bumblebee,
Ouch! He stung me!

Baa, Baa Black Sheep

(Traditional)
Baa, baa, black sheep, have you any wool?
Yes, sir, yes, sir, three bags full.
One for my master,
One for my dame,
And one for the little boy
Who lives down the lane.
Baa, baa, black sheep, have you any wool?
Yes, sir, yes, sir, three bags full.

Songs and Fingerplays for Bb *(cont.)*

Teddy Bear Action Song

(Traditional)
Teddy Bear, Teddy Bear, turn around,
Teddy Bear, Teddy Bear, touch the ground,
Teddy Bear, Teddy Bear, show your shoe,
Teddy Bear, Teddy Bear, that will do!
Teddy Bear, Teddy Bear, go upstairs,
Teddy Bear, Teddy Bear, say your prayers,
Teddy Bear, Teddy Bear, switch off the lights,
Teddy Bear, Teddy Bear, say, "Good night"!

The Bear Song

(Sing to the tune of "The Farmer in the Dell.")
The bear is in her den,
The bear is in her den,
She sleeps a lot all winter long.
The bear is in her den.

The bear is waking up,
The bear is waking up,
She stretches out her great big arms,
The bear is waking up.

The bear has two little cubs,
The bear has two little cubs,
They run around and growl and play,
The bear has two little cubs.

The bears all eat a lot,
The bears all eat a lot,
They eat so much that they get fat,
The bears all eat a lot.

The bears go in the den,
The bears go in the den,
They go to sleep all winter long,
The bears go in the den.

My Pocket Book for Bb

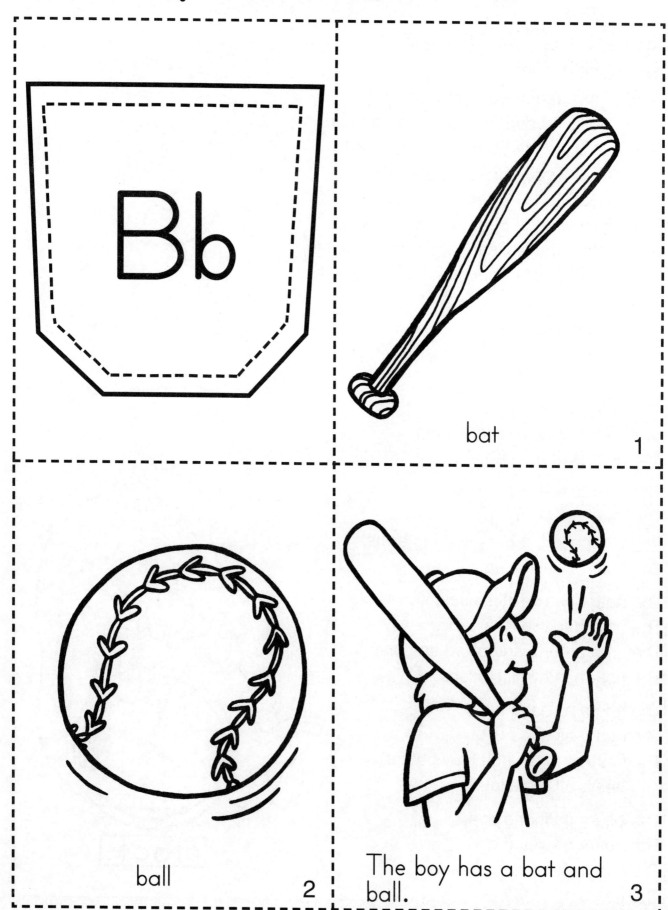

bat

1

ball

2

The boy has a bat and ball.

3

Cc

car • cat • come

Story Books

Caps for Sale by Esphyr Slobodkina
Caps, Hats, Socks, and Mittens by Louise Borden
The Cat in the Hat by Dr. Seuss
Clap Your Hands by Lorinda Bryan Cauley
Curious George by H. A. Rey
Have You Seen My Cat? by Eric Carle
If You Give a Mouse a Cookie by Laura Numeroff
Millions of Cats by Wanda Gag
Rotten Ralph by Jack Gantos
The Very Hungry Caterpillar by Eric Carle

Foods/Snacks

- cake
- candy corn
- cantaloupe
- carrots
- cat cookies, made with a cat cookie cutter
- corn bread
- cupcakes

Getting Started

1. Introduce the letter and the special picture. Read a book with the letter **C** in the title. Brainstorm a list of other words that begin with a **Cc** and write the words on a chart. Include the names of any children in the class whose names begin with **C**. (**Note:** When introducing the students to any of the activities or worksheets connected to the letter, the emphasis should be on the connection to the letter and the letter sound.)

2. Dramatize a list of action words that start with the letter **Cc**—*cut, crawl, cry, comb, climb*. Mention that an action word is also known as a "verb."

3. Label objects in the classroom that begin with the letter **Cc**—*clock, calendar, counter, crayons, cardboard, corner*, etc.

4. Play catch using balls, beanbags, or soft toys.

5. Make calendars for the month or for the year.

Language Arts for Cc

Cat Words

Materials

- *Have You Seen My Cat?* by Eric Carle
- pictures of cats
- large brown paper bags (one per child)
- yellow, red, cream, orange, brown, white, and black paint
- paintbrushes
- chart paper and marker
- strips of paper for labels
- scissors

Preparation: Remove the bottoms from the paper bags. Then cut the bags open to lay flat.

Procedure

1. Talk about cats and show pictures of various kinds and colors of cats.
2. Ask if students have cats at home and if they know about other animals in the cat family (tigers, lions, cheetahs, panthers).
3. On the chart paper, make a word map using words that describe cats.
4. Read the book, *Have You Seen My Cat?* by Eric Carle.
5. Discuss the colors and sizes of the various cats. Mention that a calico cat is a type of cat with patches of white, cream, red, and black. Most calicos are female.
6. Paint large cats on the brown paper. Give ample time for each student to paint his or her own cat pictures.
7. When dry, cut the cats out.
8. Have each student (where applicable) write or paint the word *cat* under his or her painting.
9. Ask each student to describe his or her cat, and help write a label for the painting.
10. Display the labeled paintings with the word map.

Name _____

Printing Practice for Cc

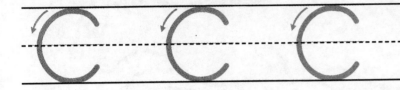

cat

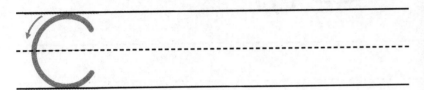

C

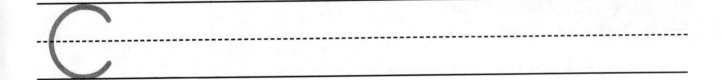

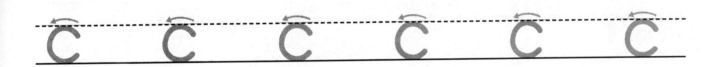

C

C

Word Practice for Cc

cat

car

come

I see the big cat.

Science Activities for Cc

Colors

Materials

- flat bottom (not cone) coffee filters (one per child)
- red, blue, and yellow food coloring
- muffin tins
- eyedroppers
- newspaper

Preparation: Put flattened coffee filters on layers of newspaper. Place red, blue, and yellow food coloring, diluted with water, in muffin tins.

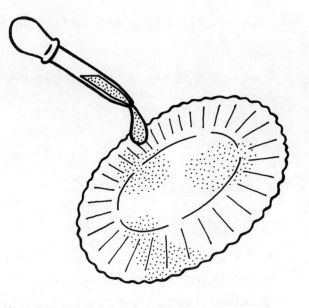

Procedure

1. Use an eyedropper to drip colors on a filter.
2. Let the colored filters dry and then display them on a window.
3. Examine what happened when colors mixed together. Focus on the blending of primary colors (red, yellow, blue) to create secondary colors (orange, green, purple). (**Suggestion:** Colored coffee filters can also be gathered into clothespins to make butterflies—see page 24.)

Camouflage

Materials

- *What Color Is Camouflage?* by Carolyn B. Otto
- old magazines or calendars
- sheets of construction paper (one per child)
- glue
- paint or colored markers
- sponges
- scissors

Procedure

1. Talk to the children about the importance of camouflage to animals. Discuss how animals are safer from their enemies when they cannot be seen in their surroundings. Explain that the animals' different colorings and habitats help hide them from other animals. For example, green lizards hide on green leaves and lion cubs are hidden in brown grasses.
2. Read the book, *What Color Is Camouflage?*
3. Cut out pictures of animals from magazines or calendars.
4. Glue the pictures on construction paper.
5. Use paint applied with sponges or markers to add or extend the background with similar colors.
6. Share the finished pictures. Find the animals in each picture.

Art Activities for Cc

Carton Caterpillars

Use this for a follow-up activity after reading *The Very Hungry Caterpillar* by Eric Carle.

Materials

- pressed-paper egg cartons (one for every two children)
- paint
- paintbrushes
- newspaper
- chenille sticks (one per child)
- markers
- scissors (for teacher)
- green paper
- sequins and decorations (optional)

Preparation: Cut each egg carton in half lengthwise to create two strips.

Procedure

1. Give each child one egg-carton strip and one chenille stick.
2. Lay the carton on the newspaper bottom-side up.
3. Paint the egg carton and let it dry.
4. Add eyes and decorations with markers.
5. Poke two holes in the head. Hook the chenille stick through the holes for antennae.
6. Display each caterpillar on a large green paper leaf.

Clown Collages

Materials

- clown pattern (page 35)
- sheets of white construction paper (one per child)
- crayons or markers
- scissors
- scraps of colored paper
- glue

Preparation: Duplicate one copy of the clown pattern onto construction paper for each student.

Procedure

1. Color the clown's face.
2. Cut or tear colored paper scraps to decorate the clown's hat.
3. Glue the colored paper pieces on the hat.
4. Give the clown a name that begins with the letter **C**.

Clown Collages

Clown Pattern

Each student will need one copy of this page.

Songs and Fingerplays for Cc

This Is the Way We Learn About Cc

(Sing to the tune of "Here We Go Round the Mulberry Bush.")

This is the way we cut the paper, cut the paper, cut the paper,

This is the way we cut the paper, we love the letter Cc!

(Repeat using the following lines.)

2nd verse—This is the way we crawl on the floor,

3rd verse—This is the way we climb a hill,

4th verse—This is the way we cry big tears,

5th verse—This is the way we come and play,

Old Gray Cat

(Author Unknown)

The old gray cat is sleeping, sleeping, sleeping.

The old gray cat is sleeping in the house.

The little mice are creeping, creeping, creeping.

The little mice are creeping in the house.

The old gray cat is waking, waking, waking.

The old gray cat is waking in the house.

The little mice go running, running, running.

The little mice go running in the house.

Variations: To enhance vocabulary development and keep the activity fresh, change the actions of the mice—dancing, hopping; and the cat—resting, stretching.

Clap, Clap, Clap Your Hands

(Sing to the tune of "Row, Row, Row Your Boat.")

Clap, clap, clap your hands as slowly as can be,

Clap, clap, clap your hands, do it now with me.

Clap, clap, clap your hands as quickly as can be,

Clap, clap, clap your hands, do it now with me.

Variations: Change the type of clapping movements to increase vocabulary and focus on different opposites—slowly/quickly; loudly/quietly. Later, when **Cc** is not the focus letter, sing the song incorporating different actions and different body parts. Here are some suggestions to get started: Stamp, stamp, stamp your feet; Tap, tap, tap your head; Wiggle, wiggle, wiggle your toes.

Songs and Fingerplays for Cc *(cont.)*

Cat Went Walking

(Author unknown)
Cat went walking, walking, walking,
Cat went walking,
Far, far away.
Cat came back again, back again, back again,
Cat came back again,
Home the same day.

Cat went creeping, creeping, creeping,
Cat went creeping,
Far, far, away.
Cat came back again, back again, back again,
Cat came back again,
Home the same day.

Cat went stalking, stalking, stalking,
Cat went stalking,
Far, far away.
Cat came back again, back again, back again,
Cat came back again,
Home the same day.

Cat went running, running, running,
Cat went running,
Far, far away.
Cat came back again, back again, back again,
Cat came back again,
Home the same day.

Caterpillar Song

(Sing to the tune of "Ten Little Indians.")
One little, two little, three little caterpillars,
Four little, five little, six little caterpillars,
Seven little, eight little, nine little caterpillars,
Chewing on a leaf!

My Pocket Book for Cc

Cc

cat

1

car

2

Come see the cat in
the car.

3

38

Dd

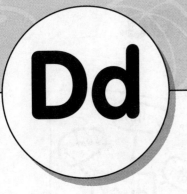

dad • dog • duck

Story Books

Dabble Duck by Anne Leo Ellis

Danny and the Dinosaur by Syd Hoff

Dinosaurs Are Different by Aliki

Doctor De Soto by William Steig

The Doorbell Rang by Pat Hutchings

Down By the Bay by Raffi

Ducks Don't Get Wet by Augusta Goldin

Go, Dog, Go by P. D. Eastman

Make Way for Ducklings by Robert McCloskey

Up, Up, Down by Robert Munsch

Foods/Snacks

- dates
- desserts
- deviled eggs
- dill pickles
- dip and chips
- dog or duck cookies, made with cookie cutters
- doughnuts

Getting Started

1. Introduce the letter and the special picture. Read a book with the letter **D** in the title. Brainstorm a list of other words that begin with a **Dd** and write the words on a chart. Include the names of any children in the class whose names begin with **D**. (**Note:** When introducing the students to any of the activities or worksheets connected to the letter, the emphasis should be on the connection to the letter and the letter sound.)

2. Play the game, Duck, Duck, Goose. Have children sit in a large circle. Choose one child to be "It." This child walks around the circle, tapping each seated child lightly on the head, and says, "Duck, duck, duck," and then he or she chooses a "Goose." The student who has been chosen as the Goose stands up and chases the other student around the circle. The It student runs until she or he can sit down in the space the Goose has vacated. If caught, the Goose sits in the center of the circle until someone else is caught.

Language Arts for Dd

Describing Words

Materials

- *Dabble Duck* by Anne Leo Ellis
- chart paper and marker
- worksheet
- pencils
- crayons

Preparation: Create a worksheet with the sentence starter, "My duck is _____." Leave space for the student to draw a picture. Duplicate a copy of the worksheet for each child.

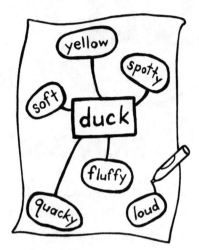

Procedure

1. Tell students that describing words (adjectives) make a story more interesting. Words that describe can be related to size, shape, color, mood, etc. Students should listen for describing words while they listen to the story.

2. Read *Dabble Duck.* Use the chart paper to make a word map of the describing words the students suggest.

3. Give each student a worksheet with the sentence starter. Have him or her fill in a describing word and draw a picture.

4. Read each sheet aloud.

5. Display students' work around the word map.

Describing Dads

Materials

- chart paper and marker
- pencils
- construction paper

Procedure

1. Discuss dads by describing what they do, what they like, and what students like about their dads. Write the students' responses on chart paper.

2. Help each student finish the sentence, "My dad is _____." Write the response on construction paper. Have each child illustrate his or her sentence.

3. Display the chart paper and the students work with the title, "Our Dads."

Name _____

Printing Practice for Dd

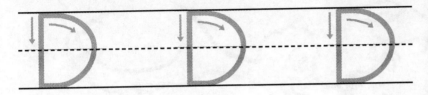

dog

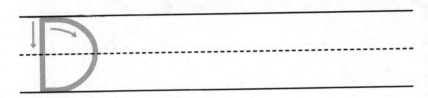

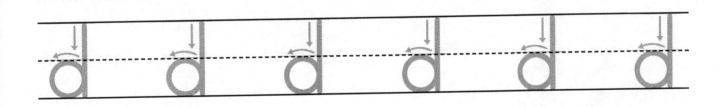

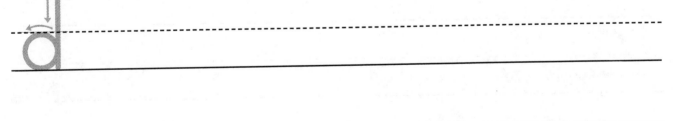

Name _____

Word Practice for Dd

dog

dad

duck

A dog sees a duck.

Science Activities for Dd

Ducks Stay Dry in the Water

Learn about ducks and why they don't get wet when they are swimming in water. Test hypotheses by doing an experiment with oil and water.

Materials

- *Ducks Don't Get Wet* by Augusta Goldin
- chart paper and marker
- brown paper squares (two per child)
- water, in a shallow dish
- vegetable oil, in a shallow dish
- two shallow dishes
- sponge brush for water
- sponge brush for oil
- spray bottle, filled with water
- scissors

Preparation: Cut out squares from large brown paper bags.

Procedure

1. Brainstorm with students why ducks do not get wet when swimming in water.
2. Write the predictions on the chart paper.
3. Read the book, *Ducks Don't Get Wet* by Augusta Goldin.
4. Dip a sponge brush in water, and "paint" one square of paper.
5. Dip a sponge brush in vegetable oil, and "paint" the other square of paper.
6. Using the spray bottle, spray water on both papers.
7. Observe what happens to the water. Relate the observation to ducks, and confirm or reject the hypotheses. Reread the predictions made by the students, and decide if their ideas were correct or not.
8. On chart paper, write conclusions about why ducks do not get wet.
9. Display the chart with the duck murals (see page 44).

Art Activities for Dd

Duck Murals

Materials

- *Ducks* by Gail Gibbons
- large sheet of butcher paper or mural paper
- blue and green watercolors
- large paintbrushes
- duck pattern (page 45)
- sheets of white construction paper (one per child)
- yellow tempera paint
- scissors
- glue
- markers

Preparation: Duplicate the duck pattern onto white construction paper for each student.

Procedure

1. Read parts of the book, *Ducks*, and point out the watercolor illustrations.
2. Divide the class into two groups. One group can paint the ducks yellow while the other group is using blue and green watercolors to paint the water on the butcher paper or mural paper. Then change the groups so all have the opportunity to do both activities.
3. Let the ducks and the watercolor background dry.
4. Cut out the ducks and glue them onto the background.
5. Use markers to add details, fish, tall grass, and lily pads.

Design Dazzling D's

Materials

- capital **D** stencil
- scissors
- newspaper
- glue
- shallow cups
- sponge brushes
- markers
- puff paint, glitter, sequins, and beads

Preparation: Pour the glue into shallow cups. Trace and cut out several **D**'s for each student.

Procedure

1. Put the **D**'s on newspaper. Use brushes to paint the **D**'s with glue.
2. Decorate using available craft materials until the **D**'s are dazzling.
3. When the **D**'s are dry, display them along with the title, "We Designed Dazzling **D**'s."

Duck Murals

Duck Pattern

Each student will need one copy of this page.

Songs and Fingerplays for Dd

Oh Where, Oh Where, Has My Little Dog Gone?

(Traditional)

Oh where, oh where, has my little dog gone,

Oh where, oh where, can he be?

With his tail so short and his ears so long,

Oh where, oh where, can he be?

Oh where, oh where, has my little dog gone,

Oh where, oh where can he be?

With his paws so big, and his fur so long,

Oh where, oh where, can he be?

Oh where, oh where, has my little dog gone,

Oh where, oh where can he be?

With his nose so short and his tongue so long,

Oh where, oh where can he be?

Little Ducky Duddle

(Traditional)

Little Ducky Duddle went wading in a puddle,

Went wading in a puddle quite small.

Said he, "It doesn't matter how much I splash and splatter,

I'm only a ducky after all. Quack, quack."

Five Little Ducks

(Traditional)

Five little ducks that I once knew,

Fat ones, skinny ones, tall ones, too.

But the one little duck with the feathers on his back,

He led the others with his "quack, quack, quack.

Quack, quack, quack."

He led the others with his "quack, quack, quack."

Down to the water they would go,

Wibble, wobble, wibble, wobble to and fro.

But the one little duck with the feathers on his back,

He led the others with his "quack, quack, quack,

Quack, quack, quack."

He led the others with a "quack, quack, quack".

(**Note:** *This song lends itself to a feltboard story.*)

Songs and Fingerplays for Dd *(cont.)*

Six Little Ducks

(Traditional)

Six little ducks went out to play,

Over the hill and far away,

Mother Duck said, "Quack, quack, quack, quack,"

Five little ducks came running back.

Five little ducks went out to play,

Over the hill and far away,

Mother Duck said, "Quack, quack, quack, quack,"

Four little ducks came running back.

Four little ducks went out to play,

Over the hill and far away,

Mother Duck said, "Quack, quack, quack, quack,"

Three little ducks came running back.

Three little ducks went out to play,

Over the hill and far away,

Mother Duck said, "Quack, quack, quack, quack,"

Two little ducks came running back.

Two little ducks went out to play,

Over the hill and far away,

Mother Duck said, "Quack, quack, quack, quack,"

But only one little duck came back.

One little duck went out to play,

Over the hill and far away,

Mother Duck said, "Quack, quack, quack, quack,"

But no little ducks came running back.

No little ducks went out to play,

Over the hill and far away,

Mother Duck said, "QUACK, QUACK, QUACK, QUACK!!!"

And all the little ducks came waddling back.

My Pocket Book for Dd

Dd

dad

1

dog

2

The dad has the dog.

3

Ee

egg • elephant • elf

Story Books

The Blind Men and the Elephant
   by Karen Backstein
Chickens Aren't the Only Ones by Ruth Heller
Elephant Crossing by Toshi Yoshida
Elmer by David McKee
The Elves and the Shoemaker by Brothers Grimm
Emmett's Pig by Mary Stolz
Horton Hatches the Egg by Dr. Seuss
The Little Engine That Could by Watty Piper
The Right Number of Elephants by Jeff Sheppard
The Story of Babar by Jean de Brunhoff

Foods/Snacks

- egg boats
  (Stick a paper flag onto a toothpick. Place each flag in half of a hard-boiled egg.)
- egg roll
- egg salad sandwiches
- eggplant
- hard-boiled eggs
- scrambled eggs

Getting Started

1. Introduce the letter and the special picture. Read a book with the letter **E** in the title. Brainstorm a list of other words that begin with an **Ee** and write the words on a chart. Include the names of any children in the class whose names begin with **E**. (**Note:** When introducing the students to any of the activities or worksheets connected to the letter, the emphasis should be on the connection to the letter and the letter sound.)

2. Have an elephant parade. Teach the students the following song:

The Elephant Song *(Sing to the tune of "Ten Little Indians.")*

   One big, two big, three great, big elephants,
   Four big, five big, six great, big elephants,
   Seven big, eight big, nine great, big elephants,
   Walking in a row.

Students stand in a circle. One student starts walking around the outside of the circle with his or her head down and hands clasped, swinging like an elephant's trunk. This "elephant" will then choose the second elephant, who will choose the third elephant and so on. Sing the song enough times so all students have the opportunity to be elephants.

Language Arts for Ee

Animals That Come from Eggs

Materials

- *Chickens Aren't the Only Ones* by Ruth Heller
- sheets of white construction paper (one per child or group)
- yellow paper
- scissors
- glue
- crayons or markers
- stapler or comb binding

Preparation: Cut large ovals from sheets of white construction paper. Glue a yellow circle in the center of each oval to represent an egg yolk. Trim the left side of the white paper so that it will be ready for binding or stapling. On the cover of the class book, write "Which Animals Come from Eggs?" Write one of these phrases on each page:

"Chickens do"   "Ducks do"   "Toads do"

"Snakes do"   "Peacocks do"   "Flies do"

"Frogs do"   "Robins do"   "Butterflies do"

"Dinosaurs did"   "Geese do"

On the last page, write, "Animals that lay eggs are called oviparous."

Procedure

1. Read the book, *Chickens Aren't the Only Ones* by Ruth Heller.
2. Ask students to recall the animals that come from eggs.
3. Distribute each page to two or three students to illustrate (in the yolk).
4. When illustrations are completed, staple or use a comb binding to put the book together. Reread the book and put in the classroom library to share.

Egg Hunt

Materials

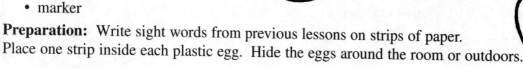

- plastic eggs
- paper strips
- marker

Preparation: Write sight words from previous lessons on strips of paper. Place one strip inside each plastic egg. Hide the eggs around the room or outdoors.

Procedure

1. Let students look for the eggs.
2. When all the eggs are found, gather the students in a circle. Take turns reading the words found in the eggs. Play again, letting a few students hide the eggs for the rest of the class to find.

Name _____

Printing Practice for Ee

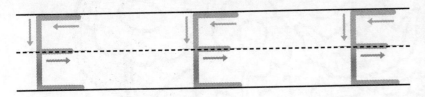

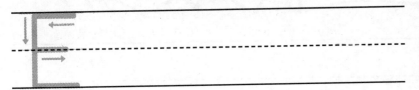

elephant

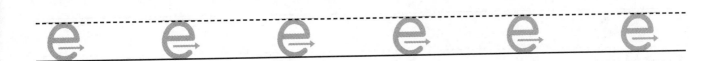

Word Practice for Ee

elephant

egg

elf

The elf is small.

Science Activities for Ee

Eggs, Eggs, Eggs!

Investigate the contents of an egg, and learn about the parts of an egg.

Materials

- raw eggs (one for every two children)
- shallow cups
- paper towels for cleanup
- chart paper and marker
- newspaper to cover the table and floor

Procedure

1. Demonstrate this activity first; be ready to help the children crack open the eggs. Crack open an egg over a shallow cup. Try to crack the egg in half. (**Suggestion:** Save the eggshells for the eggshell garden activity—see activity below.)

2. Inside the eggshell, find the membrane and gently pull it out. Look at the contents of the egg and identify the yolk and egg white.

3. Make a chart that shows the parts of an egg the students have found. Label the parts of the egg and title the chart, "We Learn About Eggs."

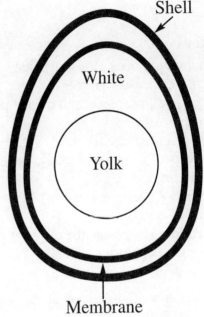

Eggshell Garden

Plant seeds in eggshell halves.

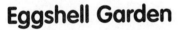

Materials

- egg cartons
- eggshell halves (one per child)
- potting soil
- fast-growing seeds (wheat berry seeds)
- spray bottle, filled with water
- slips of paper (one per child)
- funnel
- scissors

Preparation: Cut the bottom half off the egg cartons. Write each student's name on a slip of paper.

Procedure

1. Put eggshell halves in egg cartons.
2. Using a funnel, put soil in the eggshell. Gently put seeds just under the top of the soil.
3. Water with a spray bottle. Place the egg carton in a sunny window. Make a title that says, "Eggshell Garden."

Art Activities for Ee

Elephant Paintings

Learn about the habits, lifestyles, and the communal nature of the African elephant, the largest animal that lives on land.

Materials

- nonfiction book about elephants
- chart paper and marker
- gray, yellow, green, and orange paint
- paintbrushes
- elephant pattern (page 55)
- sheets of white construction paper (one per child)
- scissors
- glue
- mural paper

Preparation: Duplicate the elephant pattern onto construction paper for each child.

Procedure

1. Read a nonfiction book about elephants and discuss how elephants live in groups in the grasslands.
2. Ask students to recall some of the facts from the book and write the facts on the chart.
3. Paint the elephants with gray paint.
4. Paint the mural background to resemble the elephants' natural habitat.
5. Cut out the painted elephants.
6. Glue the elephants onto the painted background.
7. Display the mural with the chart.

Checkerboard Elephants

Materials

- *Elmer* by David McKee
- elephant pattern (page 55)
- sheets of white construction paper (one per child)
- crayons or markers

Preparation: Make one copy of the elephant pattern. Draw horizontal and vertical lines on it to look like Elmer. Duplicate this pattern onto construction paper for each child.

Procedure

1. Read the book, *Elmer* by David McKee.
2. Color the elephant using a variety of colors.
3. Display the pictures with the title, "Elephants Like Elmer."

Elephant Paintings

Elephant Pattern

For the activity, "Elephant Paintings," each student will need one copy of this page. For the activity, "Checkerboard Elephants," make one copy and follow the directions on page 54.

Songs and Fingerplays for Ee

One Little, Two Little, Three Little Elephants

(Sing to the tune of "Ten Little Indians.")

One little, two little, three little elephants,
Four little, five little, six little elephants,
Seven little, eight little, nine little elephants,
Ten little elephants standing in a row.

(**Note:** *This song adapts well to a feltboard story.*)

The Elephant

(Traditional)
The elephant goes like this and that.
(Swing arms.)
He's oh, so big.
And he's oh, so fat.
(Hold arms out.)
He has no fingers
(Clench fists.)
And he has no toes
(Clasp hands and swing.)
But goodness, gracious, what a nose!

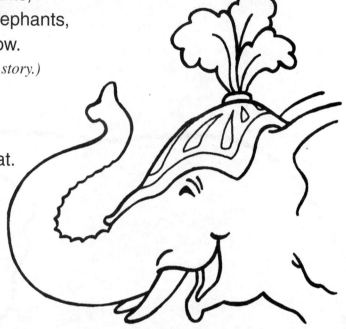

One Little Elephant Went Out to Play

(Traditional)
One little elephant went out to play
Out on a spider's web one day,
He had such enormous fun
He called for another elephant to come.
Two little elephants went out to play
Out on a spider's web one day,
They had such enormous fun
They called for another elephant to come.
Three little elephants . . .

Variation: One child is chosen to be the first elephant and walks slowly around the outside of a circle of children. When the first verse is finished, that child chooses another child to follow her or him. Continue until there are about ten students walking around the circle, and then start over with another child.

Songs and Fingerplays for Ee *(cont.)*

Down By the Station

(Traditional)

Down by the station,
Early in the morning,
All the toys are loaded,
Now it's time to go.
(Say, "But the little blue engine broke down. Who will help him?")

Down by the station
Early in the morning
See the little pufferbellies
Standing in a row.
See the stationmaster
Pull the little handle
Puff, puff, chug, chug,
Off we go.
(Say, "But will the tired old pufferbelly help? No.")

Down by the station
Early in the morning
See the big black engines
Standing in a row.
See the stationmaster
Pull the great big handle,
Wheels turn, woo, woo,
Off we go.
(Say, "But will the great big engine help? No.")

Down by the station
Early in the morning
See the friendly engine
Moving down the tracks.
(Say, "Will the friendly engine help? Yes!)
He will help the blue engine
Get over the tall mountain,
Puff, puff, chug, chug,
Here we go.
(Say, "I think I can, I think I can, I think I can. I thought I could!")

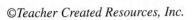

My Pocket Book for Ee

Ee

elephant

1

egg

2

The elephant sits on
an egg.

3

Ff

fast • fish • fun

Story Books

Fish Is Fish by Leo Lionni
The Foot Book by Dr. Seuss
Fossils Tell of Long Ago by Aliki
Freight Train by Donald Crews
Frog and Toad Are Friends by Arnold Lobel
Old Black Fly by Jim Aylesworth
Rainbow Fish by Marcus Pfister
The Reason for a Flower by Ruth Heller
The Story of Ferdinand by Munro Leaf
Swimmy by Leo Lionni

Foods/Snacks

- finger foods (cut-up celery, carrots or fruit)
- fish sticks
- French fries
- frosting
- fruit roll-ups
- fruit salad or slices
- fudge

Getting Started

1. Introduce the letter and the special picture. Read a book with the letter **F** in the title. Brainstorm a list of other words that begin with an **Ff** and write the words on a chart. Include the names of any children in the class whose names begin with **F**. (**Note:** When introducing the students to any of the activities or worksheets connected to the letter, the emphasis should be on the connection to the letter and the letter sound.)

2. Play the game, Find the Fish. Hide several paper fish cutouts around the room or outdoors. Have students walk around the area to find where the fish are hidden. The student who finds the most fish will hide them so the game can be played again.

3. Play a game of Fish, Fish, Frog. Play the same as Duck, Duck, Goose (see page 39) by changing the words used while walking around the circle.

Language Arts for Ff

Paper Fans With Sight Words

Materials

- 8" x 11" (20 cm x 28 cm) sheets of paper (one per child)
- pencils
- glue or stapler

Procedure

1. Make a paper fan by folding the paper back and forth across the short side.
2. Make each fold about 1" (3 cm) wide. On each layer, write a sight word such as *far, farm, fast, find, fish, foot, for, friend, from,* and *fun.*
3. Put a drop of glue on each fold or staple the folds at the bottom so the fan will be held together.
4. When the glue dries, take turns fanning each other. What does a fan do?

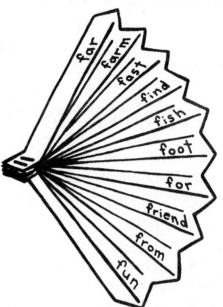

Fun for Me Book

Materials

- 12" x 18" (30 cm x 46 cm) sheets of construction paper (one per child, plus one for the cover)
- pencils
- crayons or markers
- chart paper and marker
- stapler or comb binding

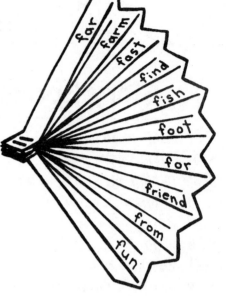

Preparation: On the construction paper, make a copy for each child with the sentence starter, "It is fun for me _____ ." Make a cover for a big book with the title, "Fun for Us."

Procedure

1. Have a class discussion about things that are fun for individual students.
2. Put the ideas in list form on a chart. Encourage students to brainstorm different and unusual ideas. Continue adding to the list.
3. After students have given their ideas, write what each student chooses to say on the line on his or her paper.
4. Use the crayons or markers to illustrate each sentence.
5. When the sheets are completed, put the book together. Have each child stand and read his or her page. Place the book in the classroom library.

It is fun for me _____ .

Printing Practice for Ff

fish

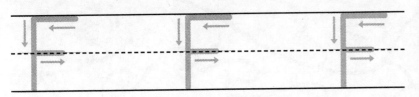

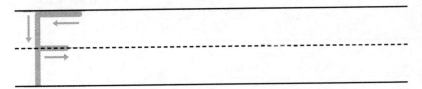

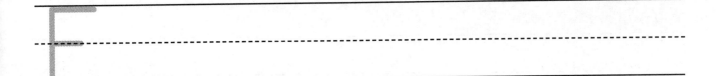

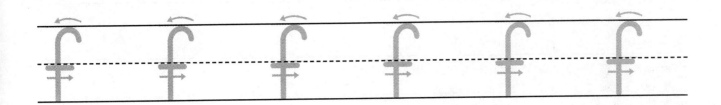

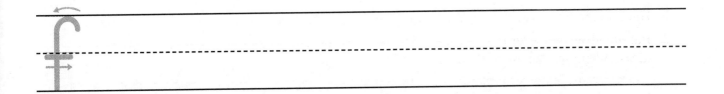

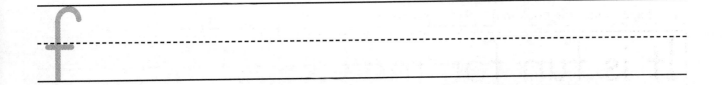

Name _____

Word Practice for Ff

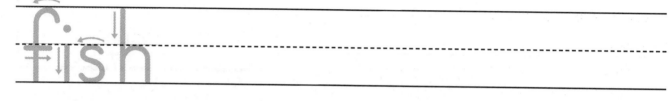

fish

fast

fun

A fish swims fast.

Science Activities for Ff

Fossils

Learn about fossils and make your own!

Materials

- *Fossils Tell of Long Ago* by Aliki
- flour
- salt
- water
- markers
- small objects (pine cones, keys, paper clips, combs)
- paper towels (one per child)
- large mixing bowl

Preparation: Make the dough using the recipe below. Mix well.

Dough Recipe (for 20–24 students)

4 cups (900 g) flour

1 cup (225 g) salt

1½ cups (360 mL) cold water

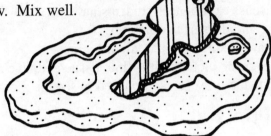

Procedure

1. Have each student write his or her name on a paper towel and set it aside.
2. Read the book, *Fossils Tell of Long Ago.*
3. Give each student a piece of dough. Demonstrate how to knead the dough; it must be kneaded for five minutes. "Push it down, fold it over."
4. When the dough is ready, flatten it and make imprints of small objects such as paper clips, keys, coins, or combs.
5. Have each student transfer the imprint to his or her labeled paper towel. Let the dough dry out. This may take several days.
6. Play a guessing game to see if other students can identify the objects used to press into the dough.

Farm Animal or Pet?

Use this classifying activity to help students discover the differences between farm animals and pets.

Materials

- old magazines
- large sheet of butcher paper

Preparation: Cut out pictures of farm animals and pets from old magazines, or download pictures of animals from your computer. Fold the butcher paper in half, open it up, and write "Farm" on one side, and "Pets" on the other.

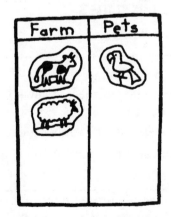

Procedure

1. Discuss why some animals are usually on a farm and some animals are pets. Farm animals provide food. Pets provide protection and companionship.
2. Show pictures of animals and identify each one. Sort the animals. Put each picture on the correct section of the butcher paper.
3. This game can be put in a learning center and made self-correcting by putting the word "Farm" or "Pet" on the back of each picture.

Art Activities for Ff

Fog Pictures

Materials

- *Hide and Seek Fog* by Alvin Tresselt
- 12" x 18" (30 cm x 46 cm) sheets of white drawing paper (one per child)
- 12" x 18" (30 cm x 46 cm) sheets of white tissue paper (one per child)
- crayons or markers
- clear tape

Procedure

1. Discuss experiences students have had with fog. Read a book about fog and discuss the pictures.
2. Draw pictures of an outdoor scene.
3. Cover the picture with white tissue and tape along the upper edge, so that the tissue can be lifted to see the picture.

Fish Prints

Materials

- *Fish Eyes: A Book You Can Count On* by Lois Ehlert
- fish, about 12" (30 cm) long, whole and frozen
- newspaper
- black paint
- white paper, large enough for the fish
- small paint roller

Preparation: Thaw the fish a little before starting the activity.

Procedure

1. Before doing this art activity, read a book that has pictures of different sizes, shapes, and colors of fish.
2. Put the fish on newspaper and paint with the roller that has been rolled in black paint. Don't use too much paint, or the details will not show.
3. Turn the fish over on the white paper and press gently all over the fish. Lift up carefully.
4. When the fish print is dry, you can add labels such as eye, gill, fin, and tail.

Foil Pictures

Materials

- aluminum foil
- poster paint
- shallow dishes or saucers
- paper
- paper towel, rubber gloves, clothespins (optional)

Preparation: Crumble the aluminum foil into balls. Pour the poster paint into shallow dishes.

Procedure

Demonstrate this activity first. Dip a foil ball in paint, wipe off excess paint on the edge of the saucer, and then stamp it down on the paper. This could also be done on an outline drawing of a fish. The painting will be similar to a sponge painting. For easier cleanup, have the students hold the tin foil with a paper towel, rubber gloves, or a clothespin.

Art Activities for Ff (cont.)

Fingerprint Pictures

Materials
- stamp pads with washable ink
- paper for printing (one per child)
- newspaper
- fine point felt tip markers

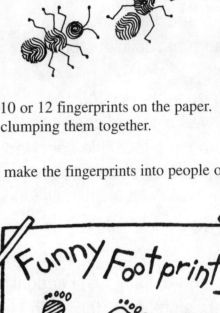

Procedure
1. Using the stamp pad and paper, have students make 10 or 12 fingerprints on the paper. Try to spread some of the prints out on the page instead of clumping them together.
2. Let the fingerprints dry.
3. Students can use fine point markers to add details to make the fingerprints into people or animals.

Footprint Mural

Materials
- *The Foot Book* by Dr. Seuss
- washable paint
- large paintbrush
- butcher paper or mural paper
- paper towels
- bucket of soapy water

Procedure
1. Read *The Foot Book* by Dr. Seuss.
2. Spread the mural paper out on the floor.
3. Have each student remove the sock and shoe from one foot.
4. Paint the bottom of the student's foot with the large paintbrush dipped in a little paint. (It tickles, be prepared for giggles!)
5. Have students walk on the mural paper to leave a footprint path.
6. After making footprints, students will wipe their feet off, dip them in the bucket of soapy water, dry them off with paper towels, and put shoes and socks back on.
7. Title your mural, perhaps with the words, "Funny Footprints."

Songs and Fingerplays for Ff

Five Speckled Frogs

(Traditional)

Five green and speckled frogs
Sittin' on a speckled log,
Eating the most delicious bugs.
Yum Yum!
One jumped into the pool,
Where it was nice and cool,
Then there were four little speckled frogs. Glub Glub!
Four green and speckled frogs . . . .
(Continue with song, with one less frog for each verse.)

Fish Story

(Traditional)

One, two, three, four, five, I caught a fish alive.
Six, seven, eight, nine, ten, then I let it go again.
Why did I let it go? Because it bit me so.
Which finger did it bite? The little finger on the right.

My Darling Little Goldfish

(Traditional)

My darling little goldfish
(Make swimming motion with hands.)
Hasn't any toes.
(Point to your toes.)
He swims around without a sound
(Make a swimming motion.)
He bumps his hungry nose.
(Put your finger on nose.)
He can't get out to play with me
(Point to self.)
Nor I get in to him.
(Shrug your shoulders.)
Although I say, "Come out and play."
(Crook your finger.)
He says, "Come in and swim."
(Make a swimming motion.)

Songs and Fingerplays for Ff *(cont.)*

The Farmer in the Dell
(Traditional)

The farmer in the dell
The farmer in the dell,
Heigh, ho, the derry-o,
The farmer in the dell.

The farmer takes a wife,
The farmer takes a wife,
Heigh, ho, the derry-o,
The farmer takes a wife.

The wife takes a child
The wife takes a child,
Heigh, ho the derry-o,
The wife takes a child

The child takes a nurse,
The child takes a nurse,
Heigh, ho the derry-o,
The child takes a nurse.

The nurse takes a dog,
The nurse takes a dog,
Heigh, ho the derry-o,
The nurse takes a dog.

The dog takes a cat,
The dog takes a cat,
Heigh, ho the derry-o,
The dog takes a cat.

The cat takes a rat,
The cat takes a rat,
Heigh, ho the derry-o,
The cat takes a rat.

The rat takes the cheese,
The rat takes the cheese,
Heigh, ho the derry-o,
The rat takes the cheese.

The cheese stands alone,
The cheese stands alone,
Heigh, ho the derry-o,
The cheese stands alone.

My Pocket Book for Ff

fish 1

fins 2

The fast fish has fins. 3

Gg

get • girl • go

Story Books

The Day the Goose Got Loose
    by Reeve Lindbergh
Go Away, Big Green Monster by Ed Emberley
Go, Dog, Go by P. D. Eastman
Good Night, Gorilla by Peggy Rathmann
Good Night Moon by Margaret Wise Brown
Grandpa and Me by Mercer Mayer
Grandpas Are for Finding Worms by Harriot Ziefert
Green Eggs and Ham by Dr. Seuss
Little Gorilla by Ruth Bornstein
Three Billy Goats Gruff by Paul Galdone

Foods/Snacks

- granola
- grapes
- green beans
- green peppers
- grilled cheese sandwiches
- gum
- gumballs

Getting Started

1. Introduce the letter and the special picture. Read a book with the letter **G** in the title. Brainstorm a list of other words that begin with a **Gg** and write the words on a chart. Include the names of any children in the class whose names begin with **G**.
   (**Note:** When introducing the students to any of the activities or worksheets connected to the letter, the emphasis should be on the connection to the letter and the letter sound.)

2. Teach the students how to gallop. Play music and let the children gallop in a large circle in the classroom or outside.

3. Label objects in the room which begin with the letter **Gg**.

4. Teach the students to play the card game, Go Fish. Put the game in a learning center to be played independently.

Language Arts for Gg

Goat Play

Materials

- *The Three Billy Goats Gruff* by Paul Galdone
- chart paper and marker
- table
- two chairs

Preparation: Arrange the chairs on either side of a low table.

Procedure

1. Ask if students have heard the story of *The Three Billy Goats Gruff* before. Ask what happened in the story they heard, and write the responses on chart paper.

2. Explain that there are different versions of the story. Read *The Three Billy Goats Gruff* by Paul Galdone.

3. Choose a child to be the troll and each of the three goats. Have the troll sit under the table.

4. Read the story again, and let the students act it out as you read. Show the goats how to cross the bridge by stepping up on the chair to the table, and then walking across the table. The troll will then pop up and shout at the goat. After answering, the first goat will step down on the other chair and go to the place designated as the green grass. Repeat the process for the second, middle-sized goat. The big goat will put his or her horns out and pretend to hit the troll when it is his or her turn on the bridge. (**Alternative:** Tell the story or have the students tell the story.)

The Goose Is Loose and Other Rhyming Words

Materials

- *The Day the Goose Got Loose* by Reeve Lindbergh
- chart paper and marker
- 5" x 8" (13 cm x 20 cm) cards

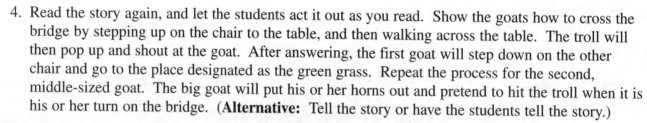

Procedure

1. Read the book, *The Day the Goose Got Loose*.

2. Then ask students to name a word that begins with **Gg** and a rhyming word, such as *green/bean, goose/moose, get/wet, go/slow, game/name, glad/sad,* and *goat/boat.*

3. Write the rhyming pairs on the chart.

4. Compare the endings and show that some rhyming words have endings that are spelled the same, and sometimes they are spelled differently.

5. Write the words on cards and match the rhyming words.

6. This activity could be put in a learning center to be used independently.

Name _____

Printing Practice for Gg

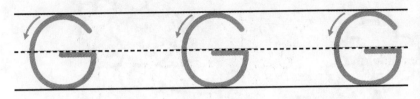

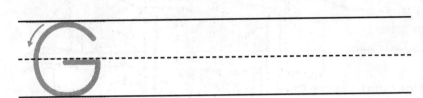

girl

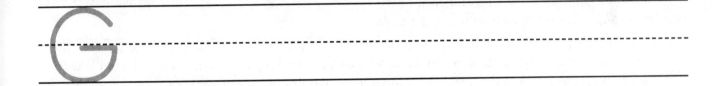

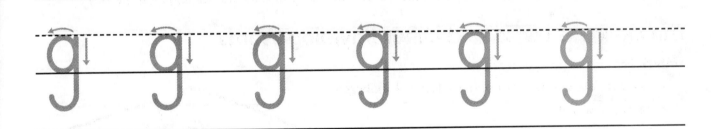

Name _____

Word Practice for Gg

girl

get

go

Go get the girl.

Science Activities for Gg

Grass Seeds

Materials

- grass seed
- potting soil
- newspaper
- spray bottle, filled with water
- tin cans (tuna fish cans)
- teaspoon (5 mL)
- strip of paper for sign

Procedure

1. Spread newspaper on the table.
2. Fill cans with 1" (3 cm) of potting soil.
3. Add a teaspoon (5 mL) of grass seed.
4. Set the cans in a sunny window.
5. Water with the spray bottle every day.
6. Add a title near the cans, "Watch Our Green Grass Garden Grow!"

Growing Green Beans

Materials

- *Growing Vegetable Soup* by Lois Ehlert
- chart paper and marker
- green bean seeds
- plastic dishpan
- plastic bottle, filled with water
- potting soil
- wooden barbeque skewers

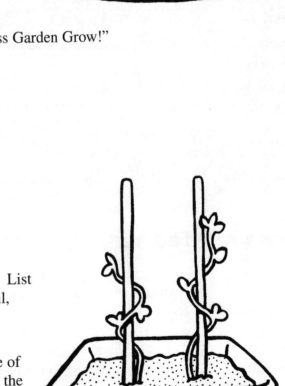

Procedure

1. Read the book and discuss how vegetables grow. List the things all green plants need to grow: sun, soil, air, and water.
2. Fill the dishpan two-thirds full with soil.
3. Plant seeds just under the surface. (**Hint:** A rule of thumb is that seeds should be planted with about the amount of soil over each seed as the seed is wide.)
4. Put a skewer next to each seed for the plant to climb on as it grows.
5. Set the dishpan in a sunny window.
6. Give the plants a small amount of water every day.
7. Divide the chart paper into eight vertical sections. Write the weekly date at the top of each section and draw a picture to keep track of what one plant looks like.
8. After the flowers have developed and dried up, little beans will begin to appear.
9. When the beans have matured, break some open to find new seeds inside the pods.

Art Activities for Gg

Glue and Glitter Gloves

Materials

- pencils
- light-colored cardstock
- glue
- glitter

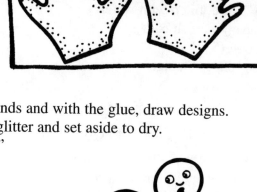

Procedure

1. Use pencils to trace right and left hands on heavy paper. Draw a line across where the wrist would be to make hands look like gloves.
2. Put a small bead of glue on the outline of the hands and with the glue, draw designs.
3. Shake glitter on the glue. Shake off the excess glitter and set aside to dry.
4. Display with the title, "Glue and Glitter Gloves."

Ghost Art

Materials

- sheets of white tissue paper (two per child)
- string
- markers

Procedure

1. Roll one of the sheets of tissue paper into a ball.
2. Put the ball in the center of the other sheet of tissue.
3. Pull the edges of the tissue paper up, and secure around the ball with string.
4. Add eyes, nose, and mouth with a marker.
5. Hang the ghosts around the room.

Geese with Feathers

Materials

- 12" x 18" (30 x 46 cm) sheets of white construction paper (one per child)
- goose pattern (page 75)
- glue
- colorful feathers (available in craft stores)

Preparation: Duplicate the goose pattern onto construction paper for each child.

Procedure

1. Distribute the goose pattern and a handful of feathers to each student.
2. Put a small drop of glue on the goose and press a feather down into it. Continue until the goose is covered with feathers.
3. Set the feather-covered goose aside to dry.
4. Display with the title, "Gorgeous Geese with Feathers."

Geese with Feathers

Goose Pattern

Each student will need one copy of this page.

Songs and Fingerplays for Gg

The Goose Is on the Loose

(Sing to the tune of "The Farmer in the Dell.")

The goose is on the loose,
The goose is on the loose,
The hens are mad, the chicks are sad,
The goose is on the loose.

Ten Little Goslings

(Sing to the tune of "Ten Little Indians.")

One little, two little, three little goslings,
Four little, five little, six little goslings,
Seven little, eight little, nine little goslings,
Ten little goslings all in a row.

The Goose Is in the Nest

(Sing to the tune of "The Farmer in the Dell.")

The egg was in the nest,
the egg was in the nest.
It was dark and stormy out,
The egg was in the nest.

The egg rolled down a hole,
The egg rolled down a hole.
It rolled into a woodchuck hole,
The egg rolled down a hole.

A goose hatched out of the egg,
A goose hatched out of the egg.
It swam and played but was really sad,
A goose hatched out of the egg.

The goose learned how to fly,
The goose learned how to fly.
Now he's happy in the sky,
The goose learned how to fly.

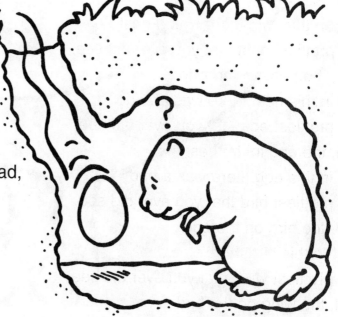

Songs and Fingerplays for Gg *(cont.)*

The Green Grass Grew All Around

(Traditional)

There was a hole in the middle of the ground

The prettiest hole that you ever did see.

Well, the hole in the ground

And the green grass grew all around all around

And the green grass grew all around.

(Add each verse and sing the last two lines.)

And in this hole there was a root

The prettiest root that you ever did see.

Well, the root in the hole . . .

And on this root there was a tree

The prettiest tree that you ever did see.

Well, the tree on the root . . .

And on this tree, there was a branch

The prettiest branch that you ever did see.

Well, the branch on the tree . . .

And on this branch there was a twig

The prettiest twig that you ever did see.

Well, the twig on the branch . . .

And on this twig there was a nest

The prettiest nest that you ever did see.

Well, the nest on the twig . . .

And in this nest there was an egg

The prettiest egg that you ever did see.

Well, the egg in the nest . . .

And in this egg there was a bird

The prettiest bird that you ever did see.

Well, the bird on the egg . . .

And on this bird there was a wing

The prettiest wing that you ever did see.

Well, the wing on the bird . . .

And on this wing there was a feather

The prettiest feather that you ever did see.

Well, the feather on the wing . . .

My Pocket Book for Gg

girl 1

grass 2

The girl will grow grass. 3

Hh

hand • hat • his

Story Books

Caps, Hats, Socks, and Mittens: A Book About the Four Seasons by Louise Borden
The Cat in the Hat by Dr. Seuss
Happy Birthday, Moon by Frank Asch
Harold and the Purple Crayon by Crockett Johnson
The Happy Hippopatami by Bill Martin, Jr.
Harry the Dirty Dog by Gene Zion
The Hat by Jan Brett
Here Are My Hands by Bill Martin, Jr.
A House for Hermit Crab by Eric Carle
Jennie's Hat by Ezra Jack Keats
Little Red Hen by Paul Galdone

Foods/Snacks

- candy hearts
- cereal with holes
- ham
- honey
- honeydew melon
- hot chocolate
- hot dogs

Getting Started

1. Introduce the letter and the special picture. Read a book with the letter **H** in the title. Brainstorm a list of other words that begin with an **Hh** and write the words on a chart. Include the names of any children in the class whose names begin with **H**. (**Note:** When introducing the students to any of the activities or worksheets connected to the letter, the emphasis should be on the connection to the letter and the letter sound.)

2. Have a hoop activity. Hoops can be purchased to use year after year. Or, ask students to bring hoops from home. Take students to the gym or outdoors. Spin the hoops and try to keep them up with hip action. Put hoops on the ground and follow directions:

   - hop on one foot inside the hoop
   - hop on one foot outside the hoop
   - jump on two feet inside the hoop
   - stand inside and jump out of the hoop
   - put hoop over head and let it fall
   - put hoop on ground and pull it up over head

Language Arts for Hh

Hats of Many Colors

Materials

- *Blue Hat, Green Hat* by Sandra Boynton
- red, orange, yellow, green, blue, purple, brown, and black paint
- paintbrushes
- paper plates (one per child)
- index cards

Preparation: On each index card, write one of the following phrases: *red hat, orange hat, yellow hat, green hat, blue hat, purple hat, brown hat, black hat.*

Procedure

1. Read the book, *Blue Hat, Green Hat.*

2. Paint the paper plates so that there are two or three of each color.

3. Write a take-off book about the hats and colors. (**Note:** Take-off books are written using the same sentence patterns as the original book. A word or two are changed. If the text says, "Mary wore her red hat," a take-off book might say, "Mary wore her yellow dress.")

4. Dramatize the story using the paper plates as hats.

5. Add the paper plates and the word cards to a learning center where students can match each card to the corresponding paper plate.

Happiness

Materials

- a book about feelings
- chart paper and marker
- strips of paper (one per child)
- crayons or markers

Preparation: On each strip of paper, write the sentence starter, "I am happy when . . . ."

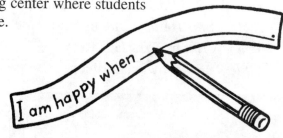

Procedure

1. Show an object that makes you (the teacher) happy, perhaps a flower, a new box of markers, or a beautiful picture. Tell the students that the object makes you happy.

2. Read a book about feeling happy.

3. Write the word "Happy" in the center of the chart paper. As students state what makes them happy, write their suggestions on the chart.

4. Distribute the prepared sentence strips. Help students complete the sentence.

5. Have each student illustrate her or his sentence strip.

6. Display the pictures with the sentence strips and the title, "Happiness is . . . ."

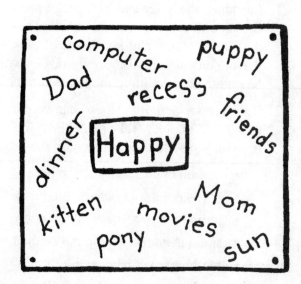

Name _____

Printing Practice for Hh

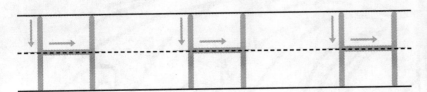

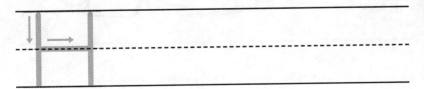

hat

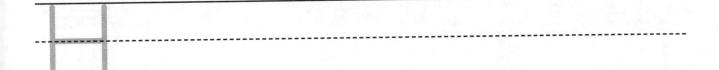

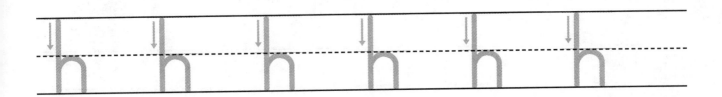

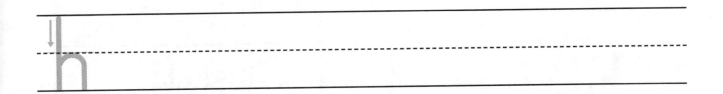

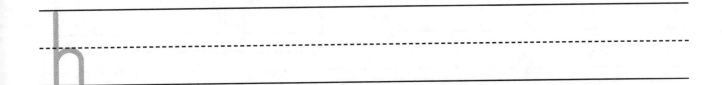

Name _____

Word Practice for Hh

hat

hand

his

This is his hat.

Science Activities for Hh

Habitats

Read a nonfiction book about animal habitats. Create a game matching animals to their homes.

Materials

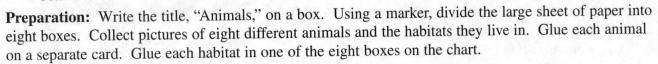

- *A House Is a House for Me* by Mary Ann Hoberman
- pictures of animals on cards
- pictures of animal homes
- large sheet of paper
- box

Preparation: Write the title, "Animals," on a box. Using a marker, divide the large sheet of paper into eight boxes. Collect pictures of eight different animals and the habitats they live in. Glue each animal on a separate card. Glue each habitat in one of the eight boxes on the chart.

Procedure

1. Identify the animal homes on the large sheet of paper. Do the same with the pictures of animals.
2. Match the animals to the animal homes. Put the animal card in the correct box on the habitat chart.
3. This game may be made self-correcting by putting a small picture of the habitat on the back of each animal card.

Harry's Hairy Head

Grow "hair" on Harry's head by planting seeds and watching them grow.

Materials

- soup cans (one per child)
- potting soil
- fast-growing seeds (wheat berry or radishes)
- strips of paper (one per child)
- crayons or markers
- glue
- water
- teaspoon

Preparation: Empty and wash out the soup cans. Cut strips of paper to cover each can.

Procedure

1. Draw eyes, mouth, nose, and ears on the center of the strip of paper.
2. Fill can with potting soil up to 1" (3 cm) from the top.
3. Add a teaspoon (5 mL) of seeds to the soil. Poke them gently into the soil.
4. Glue the strip of paper on the can.
5. Water the soil and seeds.
6. Set the can in a sunny window. Watch Harry's hair grow!
7. When the seeds begin to grow, put a sign near the cans that says, "Harry is happy. He has hair."

Art Activities for Hh

Handprints

Materials

- *Here Are My Hands* by Bill Martin, Jr.
- sheets of white construction paper (one per child)
- red, yellow, and blue poster paint
- paintbrushes
- paper towels
- water
- plastic trays (one per color)

Procedure

1. Read the book, *Here Are My Hands*.
2. Use a paintbrush to paint the bottom of a tray.
3. Press the left and right hands into the paint.
4. Press each hand on the paper. Make several prints in several colors.
5. Wipe the excess paint off hands using paper towels.
6. Rinse hands after each color.
7. When dry, hang the paintings with the title, "Here Are Our Hands."

Horses on a Hill

Materials

- horse pattern (page 85)
- large sheet of mural or butcher paper
- white construction paper (one per child)
- crayons or markers
- glue
- scissors
- paintbrushes
- green paint

Preparation: Duplicate the horse pattern onto white paper for each student.

Procedure

1. Paint a hill on the mural paper using green paint.
2. Color and cut out the horses.
3. Glue the horses on the hill.
4. Display the mural with the title, "Horses on a Hill."

Horses on a Hill

Horse Pattern

Each student will need one copy of this page.

Songs and Fingerplays for Hh

Humpty Dumpty

(Nursery Rhyme)

Humpty Dumpty sat on a wall,
Humpty Dumpty had a great fall.
All the king's horses
And all the king's men
Couldn't put Humpty Dumpty together again.

Hickory Dickory Dock

(Nursery Rhyme)

Hickory, dickory, dock
The mouse ran up the clock.
The clock struck one,
And down he ran,
Hickory, dickory dock.
Tick, tock!

Hush Little Baby

(Traditional)

Hush little baby, don't say a word
Mama's going to buy you a mockingbird.
If that mockingbird won't sing,
Papa's going to buy you a diamond ring.
If that diamond ring turns brass,
Mama's going to buy you a looking glass.
If that looking glass gets broke,
Mama's going to buy you a billy goat.
If that billy goat won't pull,
Mama's going to buy you a cart and mule.
If that cart and mule turn over,
Mama's going to buy you a dog named Rover.
If that dog named Rover won't bark,
Mama's going to buy you a horse and cart.
If that horse and cart fall down,
You'll still be the sweetest baby in town.

Songs and Fingerplays for Hh *(cont.)*

Hokey Pokey

(Traditional)

You put your right hand in,
You take your right hand out,
You put your right hand in,
And you shake it all about.
Do the Hokey Pokey and you turn yourself around.
That's what it's all about!

You put your left hand in,
You take your left hand out,
You put your left hand in,
And you shake it all about.
Do the Hokey Pokey and you turn yourself around.
That's what it's all about!

You put your right foot in,
You take your right foot out,
You put your right foot in,
And you shake it all about.
Do the Hokey Pokey and you turn yourself around.
That's what it's all about!

You put your left foot in,
You take your left foot out,
You put your left foot in,
And you shake it all about.
Do the Hokey Pokey and you turn yourself around.
That's what it's all about!

You put your right hip in,
You take your right hip out,
You put your right hip in.
And you shake it all about,
Do the Hokey Pokey and you turn yourself around.
That's what it's all about!

(Add other body parts.)

My Pocket Book for Hh

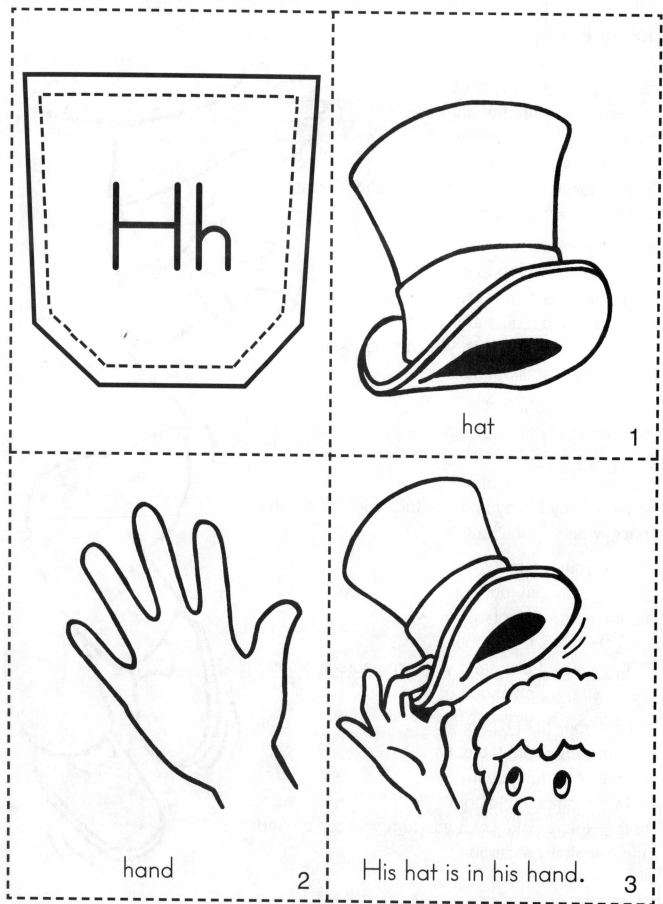

Hh

hat

1

hand

2

His hat is in his hand.

3

insect • is • it

Story Books

If You Take a Mouse to the Movies
   by Laura Joffe Numeroff

Imogene's Antlers by David Small

Insects Are My Life by Megan MacDonald

Is It Red? Is It Yellow? Is It Blue? by Tana Hoban

It Could Always Be Worse by Margot Zemach

Itchy, Itchy Chicken Pox by Grace Maccarone

It's Raining, It's Pouring by Andrea Spaulding

Jingle Dancer by Cynthia Leitich Smith

The Legend of the Bluebonnet by Tomie dePaola

The Legend of the Indian Paintbrush
   by Tomie dePaola

Foods/Snacks

- celery stick for **i**, raisin for dot
- gummy candy worm "inchworms"
- insect cookies, six pretzel sticks stuck into marshmallows
- instant pudding

Getting Started

1. Introduce the letter and the special picture. Read a book with the letter **I** in the title. Brainstorm a list of other words that begin with an **Ii** and write the words on a chart. Include the names of any children in the class whose names begin with **I**. (**Note:** When introducing the students to any of the activities or worksheets connected to the letter, the emphasis should be on the connection to the letter and the letter sound.)

2. Teach "The Inchworm Song" on page 97. Tape-record the students singing the song.

3. Dramatize inchworm movements. Have students lie down on their tummies. They should move their feet up as far as possible, then walk their hands out in front. Play the prerecorded song for the students while they move like inchworms.

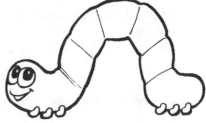

4. Write the initials of each student on drawing paper. Discuss how an initial is the first letter of a name, and the purpose of initials. Decorate each sheet of initials and display with the title, "Individuals Have Initials."

Language Arts for Ii

Imagine That!

Materials

- paper for background of collage
- scraps of colored paper
- scraps of yarn, ribbon, fabric, and crepe paper
- glue
- scissors
- chart paper and marker

Preparation: On the chart paper, write the title, "It Is Fun to Use Your Imagination." Write "Ideas" under the title.

Procedure

1. Discuss using your imagination. Tell the students about something you imagine.
2. Let students choose materials to make collages on paper.
3. Display student imaginative creations with the chart.

Initial Poems

Materials

- sheets of white construction paper (one per child)
- example of an Initial Poem
- crayons or markers

Preparation: On a sheet of construction paper, write each student's initials down the left side. Write an example of an initial poem, perhaps using your own initials. For example: CLH

Procedure

1. Share the example of an acrostic poem.
2. Help students think of words that would describe characteristics.
3. Write the words after each student's initials after he or she shares descriptive words.
4. Decorate the poem page.
5. Display the student work with the title, "Initials Are Important."

Interviews

Materials

- none, students will need time and opportunities to interview people

Procedure

1. Discuss interviewing. Plan questions students can ask.
2. Interview school helpers.
3. Take turns giving oral reports on the results of the interviews.

Name _____

Printing Practice for Ii

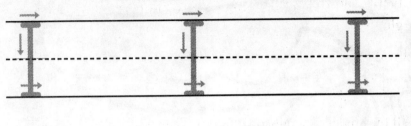

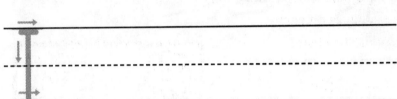

insect

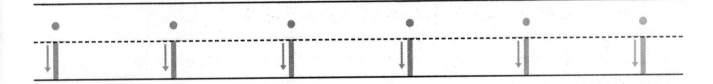

Word Practice for Ii

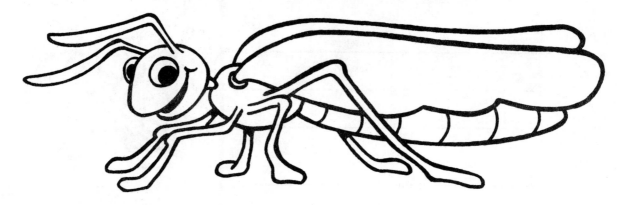

insect

it

is

It is an insect.

92

Science Activities for Ii

Insects

Learn about the characteristics of insects.

Materials

- variety of picture books about insects
- large sheets of construction paper (one per child)
- crayons or markers
- chart paper and marker
- stapler, comb bindings or rings

Procedure

1. Share pictures of a variety of insects.
2. Discuss the characteristics of insects (three body parts, six legs, two antennae).
3. List the characteristics on chart paper. Mention that insects may have wings.
4. Draw insects using the pictures and books as a resource.
5. Put the class insect pages together and create a cover for the book. Bind the pages together.
6. Select a name for each insect and write it under the picture.
7. Read the new book and add it to the classroom library.

It's Raining

Learn about the water cycle. Rain comes from the clouds. Water evaporates and becomes water vapor. Water vapor becomes clouds.

Materials

- *It's Raining, It's Pouring* by Andrea Spaulding
- chart paper and marker
- tea kettle
- chilled plate
- paper towel

Procedure

1. Ask students to share ideas about rain.
2. Write their ideas on chart paper.
3. Read a book that describes the water cycle, such as *It's Raining, It's Pouring*.
4. Boil water in a tea kettle.
5. Hold a chilled plate over the steam from the spout. Show the condensation on the bottom of the plate.
6. Wipe off some of the water. Let students feel that the towel is wet.
7. Draw a picture of the water cycle on the chart paper.

Art Activities for Ii

Inkblot Pictures

Materials

- 9" x 12" (23 cm x 30 cm) sheets of drawing paper (one per child)
- ink or dark paint
- teaspoon
- newspaper

Preparation: Fold the sheets of paper in half. Put the drawing paper on plenty of newspaper.

Procedure

1. Put a teaspoon of ink on one side of the paper.
2. Fold the paper and rub your hand over the paper to spread the paint.
3. Open the folded paper and let it dry.
4. Look at the inkblot. Encourage students to use their imagination to decide what each inkblot looks like.
5. Write a title on each inkblot picture.

Icky Insects

Materials

- *The Icky Bug Alphabet Book* by Jerry Pallotta
- insect patterns (page 95)
- crayons or markers

Preparation: Duplicate a copy of the insect patterns for each student.

Procedure

1. Read the book and discuss why some people think bugs are "icky."
2. Color the insects and display with the title, "Icky Insects."

Icky Insects

Insect Patterns

Each student will need one copy of this page.

Songs and Fingerplays for Ii

I'm a Little Teapot

(Traditional)

I'm a little teapot,
Short and stout.
Here is my handle,
Here is my spout.
When I get all steamed up,
Here me shout,
Just tip me over and pour me out.

I'm a very clever pot
That's true
Here's an example
Of what I can do.
I can change my handle
And my spout.
Just tip me over and pour me out!

It's Raining

(Traditional)

It's raining, it's pouring,
The old man is snoring.
He went to bed with a cold in his head,
And didn't get up until morning.

Itsy Bitsy Spider

(Traditional)

The itsy bitsy spider went up the water spout.
Down came the rain and washed the spider out.
Out came the sun and dried up all the rain,
And the itsy bitsy spider went up the spout again.

Songs and Fingerplays for Ii (cont.)

The Inchworm Song

(Sing to the tune of "The Wheels on the Bus.")

The inchworm on the branch goes inch by inch,
Inch by inch,
Inch by inch.
The inchworm on the branch goes inch by inch,
All day long.

The inchworm on the leaf goes inch by inch,
Inch by inch,
Inch by inch.
The inchworm on the leaf goes inch by inch,
All day long.

The inchworm on the grass goes inch by inch,
Inch by inch,
Inch by inch.
The inchworm on the grass goes inch by inch,
All day long.

The inchworm on the twig goes inch by inch,
Inch by inch,
Inch by inch.
The inchworm on the twig goes inch by inch,
All day long.

My Pocket Book for Ii

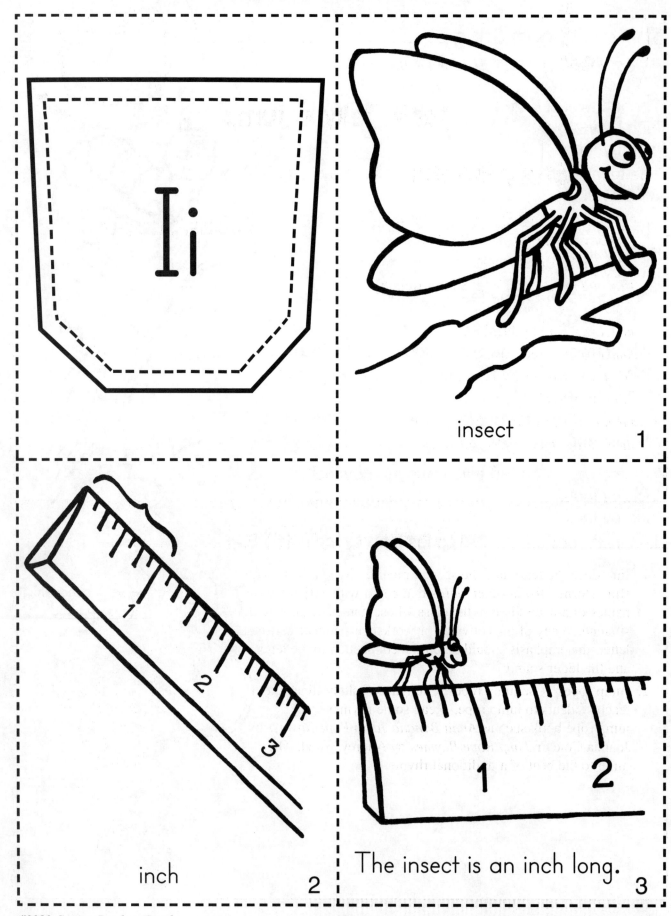

Ii

insect
1

inch
2

The insect is an inch long.
3

Jj

jar • jelly • jump

Story Books

Bread and Jam for Frances by Russell Hoban

The Day Jimmy's Boa Ate the Wash
   by Trinka Hakes Noble

Jack and the Beanstalk by Steven Kellogg

Jamaica Tag-Along by Juanita Havill

Jamaica's Find by Juanita Havill

Jamberry by Bruce Degan

The Jolly Postman by Janet and Allen Ahlberg

Julius by Angela Johnson

Jumanji by Chris Van Allsburg

Jump, Frog, Jump by Robert Kalan

Foods/Snacks

- ice cubes made from juice
- jam
- jelly
- jelly beans
- juice

Getting Started

1. Introduce the letter and the special picture. Read a book with the letter **J** in the title. Brainstorm a list of other words that begin with a **Jj** and write the words on a chart. Include the names of any children in the class whose names begin with **J**. (**Note:** When introducing the students to any of the activities or worksheets connected to the letter, the emphasis should be on the connection to the letter and the letter sound.)

2. Jump ropes. Use jump ropes or lengths of clothesline and teach students to jump rope. Read some rhymes from a jump rope book such as *Anna Banana Jump Rope Rhymes* by Joanna Cole or *Jump Rope Rhymes* by Audrey Wood. Or, jump to the beat of a traditional rhyme.

Language Arts for J j

Joke-Telling Party

Materials

- *Ready, Set, Read and Laugh!* by Stephanie Calmenson
- 5" x 8" (13 cm x 20 cm) cards
- strip of paper and marker
- string
- snack that begins with the letter **Jj**

Preparation: Write a joke on each card. Write "Joker" on the strip of paper to make a sign. Attach string to the sign.

Procedure

1. Read some jokes from the joke book for children and discuss why jokes are funny.
2. Distribute cards with jokes on them and help students read and learn the jokes.
3. Invite another class to come and share a fun experience.
4. Put the "Joker" sign over one student's head to indicate it is his or her turn to tell a joke.
5. Share the snack.

Jack and Jill

Materials

- "Jack and Jill" poem (page 106)
- pail
- table
- two chairs
- chart paper and marker

Preparation: Write the poem, "Jack and Jill" on chart paper. Place one chair at each end of the table to create a "hill."

Procedure

1. Read the poem, "Jack and Jill" on page 106.
2. Point out the rhyming words in the poem (*Jill, hill; down, crown*). Show that the endings are spelled the same.
3. Have two students dramatize the poem while the rest of the class recites it.
4. Jack and Jill will hold the pail, step up on a chair, up to the table, step down on the other chair, and carefully fall down on the floor.

Jumping Jacks and Jogging

Materials

- two strips of paper and marker

Preparation: Write the phrase, "Jumping Jacks" on one strip of paper. Write the word, "Jog" on the other strip of paper.

Procedure

1. Teach the words "Jumping Jacks" and "Jog."
2. Teach the students how to do jumping jacks and jogging.
3. Go to the gym or outside and tell the students to do what the sign says. Hold up one sign at a time so the students can follow directions by reading the words.

Name _____

Printing Practice for J j

jar

J   J   J

J

J

j   j   j   j   j   j

j

j

Name _____

Word Practice for J j

j a r

j u m p

j e l l y

Jack likes to jump.

Science Activities for Jj

Jar Garden

Create a terrarium in a jar.

Materials
- large jars with lids
- charcoal
- potting soil
- small plants or seeds
- water
- towels or foam

Preparation: Pound the charcoal into small bits and pieces.

Procedure
1. Turn the jar on its side.
2. Put a layer of charcoal in the bottom.
3. Add a layer of soil.
4. Gently plant the roots of a few small plants into the soil, or add seeds.
5. Add ¼ cup (120 mL) water to the soil to start.
6. Put the lid on, and rest the jar on a towel so it will not roll.
7. Watch to see if the jar garden has the right amount of water. Condensation should form, but the soil should be quite dry so the plants will not have too much water.

Jellyfish

Learn interesting facts about jellyfish.

Materials

- *Jellyfish* by Leighton Taylor or *Jellies: The Life of a Jellyfish* by Twig C. George
- chart paper and marker
- watercolor paints
- paintbrushes
- paper for painting (one per child)

Procedure
1. Show the cover of one of the books or a picture of a jellyfish. Ask what students already know about jellyfish. Write the ideas on chart paper.
2. Read one of the nonfiction books suggested to learn more about jellyfish. Ask students what they have learned about jellyfish. Add this new information to the chart. Note the pictures that show transparent jellyfish.
3. Demonstrate using watercolors to keep a painting transparent.
4. Paint pictures of jellyfish.
5. Let the paintings dry.
6. Review the chart and display it with the paintings.

Art Activities for J j

Jewelry Making

Materials

- plastic or wooden beads
- elastic string
- small containers, to hold the beads

Preparation: Divide the beads into small containers. Cut the elastic string so it is long enough for a necklace or bracelet. Make enough for one per child.

Procedure

1. Distribute the containers of beads.
2. Distribute the elastic strings. Tie one bead at one end so that the beads will not fall off.
3. Put the string through the holes.
4. Tie the ends of the string together.
5. Display with a sign, "Our Jewelry."

Jack-in-the-Box Puppets

Materials

- milk cartons, quart (946 ml)
- Jack pattern (page 105)
- white construction paper
- colored construction paper
- glue
- scissors
- craft sticks
- crayons or markers

Preparation: Wash out, cut off two sides of the tops, and cut slits in the bottoms of the milk cartons. Duplicate a copy of the Jack pattern onto white construction paper for every two children.

Procedure

1. Color and cut out the Jack pattern.
2. Cut a rectangle of construction paper to fit around the milk carton.
3. Glue the rectangle of colored construction paper around the milk carton.
4. Glue the Jack cutout to the craft stick.
5. Slip the stick through the slit in the bottom of the carton.
6. Push the stick up to make Jack jump out of the carton.
7. While having Jack jump out of the box, recite the poem on the pattern.

Jumping Jack

Jack is nimble
Jack jumps high
Jack jumps out
Touches the sky.

Jack-in-the-Box Puppets

Jack Pattern

For every two children, you will need one copy of this page.

Jumping Jack

Jack is nimble.
Jack jumps high.
Jack jumps out
and touches the
sky.

Jumping Jack

Jack is nimble.
Jack jumps high.
Jack jumps out
and touches the
sky.

Songs and Fingerplays for Jj

Jack and Jill
(Traditional)

Jack and Jill went up the hill
To fetch a pail of water.
Jack fell down and broke his crown
And Jill came tumbling after.

Jack Be Nimble
(Traditional)

Jack, be nimble,
Jack be quick.
Jack jumped over the candlestick.

Jack Sprat
(Traditional)

Jack Sprat could eat no fat,
His wife could eat no lean.
And so, between the two of them,
They licked the platter clean.

Little Jack Horner
(Traditional)

Little Jack Horner
Sat in a corner
Eating his Christmas pie.
He put in his thumb
And pulled out a plum
And said, "What a good boy am I!"

John Jacob Jingleheimer Schmidt
(Traditional)

John Jacob Jingleheimer Schmidt
(Point outward.)
His name is my name too!
(Point to self.)
Whenever we go out
(Shrug shoulders.)

The people always shout
(Put hands around mouth.)
There goes John Jacob
Jingleheimer Schmidt!
La da da da da da da
(Point outward.)

Songs and Fingerplays for J j *(cont.)*

Jim Along Josie

(Traditional)

Hey, Jim along, Jim along Josie
(Walk in a circle.)
Hey, Jim along, Jim along Joe.
Chorus:
Turn to the center,
Hands on your knees,
Jump three times
And turn around, please.

(Variations:)

Tip-toe along, tip-toe along Josie
Tip-toe along, Jim along Joe.
(Repeat chorus.)
Hey, jog along, jog along Josie
Hey, jog along, jog along Joe.
(Repeat chorus.)

Jack in the Box Song

(Sing to the tune of "Frere Jacques.")

Jack in the box, Jack in the box,
Are you there? Are you there?
Are you hiding
Way down in the dark?
In the dark,
In the dark?
Jack in the box, Jack in the box,
Are you there? Are you there?
You can come out here now,
You can come out here now.
We miss you
We miss you.

(Jack pops out.)

Jack in the box, Jack in the box,
Here you are. Here you are.
We are glad to see you,
We are glad to see you
Stay out here,
Stay out here.

My Pocket Book for Jj

J j

jump   1

jar   2

John jumps to get the jar.   3

Kk

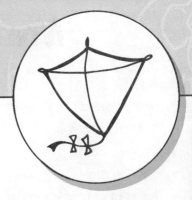

kick • kiss • kite

Story Books

Counting Kisses by Karen Katz

Curious George Flies a Kite
  by H. A. Rey, Margret Rey

Jump, Kangaroo, Jump by Stuart J. Murphy

The Kangaroo by Sabrina Crewe

A Kiss for Little Bear
  by Else Holmelund Minarik

The Kissing Hand by Audrey Penn

Koala Lou by Mem Fox

Komodo! by Peter Sis

The Tale of Tom Kitten by Beatrix Potter

What Do You Do with a Kangaroo? by Mercer Mayer

Foods/Snacks

• fruit kabobs
• ketchup
• key lime pie
• kiwi fruit

Getting Started

1. Introduce the letter and the special picture. Read a book with the letter **K** in the title. Brainstorm a list of other words that begin with a **Kk** and write the words on a chart. Include the names of any children in the class whose names begin with **K**. (**Note:** When introducing the students to any of the activities or worksheets connected to the letter, the emphasis should be on the connection to the letter and the letter sound.)

2. Play a game of kickball. You will need a playground ball. Go to the gym or outside. Kickball is played like baseball with a home plate and three bases. Divide the class in half. Half will be in line for a turn to kick, and the other half is out in the field. The pitcher rolls the ball to home plate and the student kicks the ball. When a student in the field picks up the ball, he or she tries to tag the runner with it. To make the game more appropriate for young students, they can only run to one base at a time. If they are tagged with the ball, they go to the end of the line and wait for a turn to kick.

3. Use ketchup as fingerpaint, and write **Kk**'s.

4. Make designs using dried kidney beans.

Language Arts for Kk

Materials

- *Jump, Kangaroo, Jump* by Stuart J. Murphy or *What Do You Do with a Kangaroo?* by Mercer Mayer
- measuring tape
- masking tape
- sheets of construction paper (one per child)
- crayons or markers
- stapler or binder rings

Preparation: On each sheet of construction paper, write the words, "Jump, _____, jump!"

Procedure

1. Tell about kangaroos and how far they can jump. Mention that their strong back legs let them jump up to 30 feet (910 cm) and they can hop up to 40 miles (64 km) per hour.
2. Read a book about kangaroos.
3. Put tape on the floor to show where the kangaroo would start jumping.
4. Use the measuring tape to measure 30 feet (910 cm). Compare the distance a kangaroo can jump with that of the students' jumps.
5. Help the students write the word *kangaroo* on the line on the paper and draw a picture to go with the sentence.
6. Using a stapler or binding rings, bind the pages together to make a class book.
7. As a class, read the book and have each child read his or her page.

Kangaroos Jump, Birds Fly

Materials

- chart paper and marker
- pictures of animals
- picture of a kangaroo

Procedure

1. Discuss the idea that animals move in different ways.
2. Show a picture of a kangaroo, and use a word to describe how that animal moves. Discuss other animals, share pictures, and compare their movements.
3. On the chart, write the name of the animal share pictures, and the action word a student suggests. For example, "Kangaroos jump. Birds fly. Dogs run. Fish swim. Cats creep. Rabbits hop."
4. Imitate movements of the animals while singing a song to the tune of "Here We Go 'Round the Mulberry Bush." For example, "We can jump like kangaroos jump, kangaroos jump . . . on a sunny day."

Name _____

Printing Practice for Kk

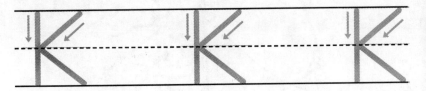

kite

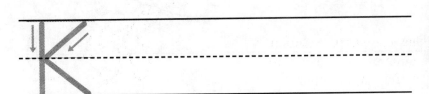

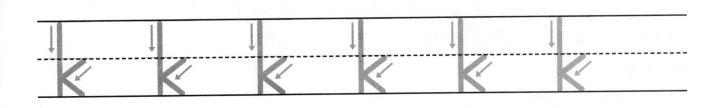

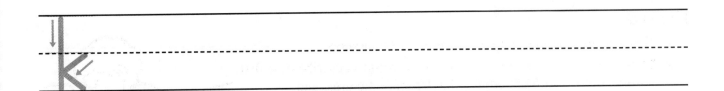

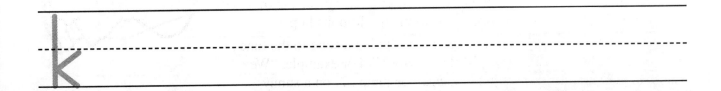

Name _____

Word Practice for Kk

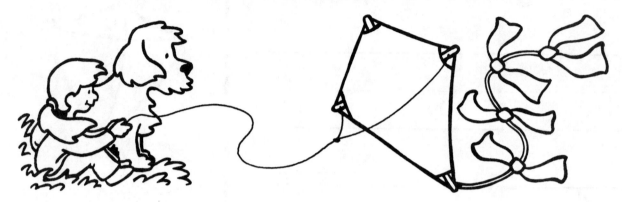

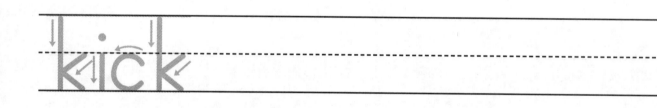
kite

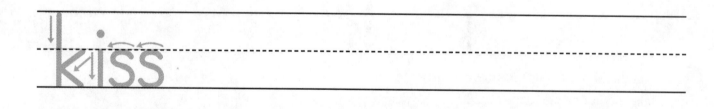
kick

kiss

We will fly a kite.

Science Activities for Kk

Koalas and Kangaroos: Australian Animals

Materials
- map of the world
- *Kangaroo* by Sabrina Crewe and *Koala Lou* by Mem Fox
- chart paper and marker
- measuring tape
- two large cards

Preparation: Locate books about Australian animals. (Many pictures and articles about Australian animals can be found on the Internet.) Write the word *kangaroo* on one large card, and *koala* on the other card.

Procedure

1. Show a large map of the world and find Australia.

2. Explain that scientists think Australian animals are unusual because Australia is an island.

3. Read the books about kangaroos and koalas.

4. Write facts about the animals on the chart paper. A kangaroo can hop up to 40 miles (64 km) per hour and can jump up to 30 feet (910 cm). Koalas live in trees and eat eucalyptus leaves.

5. Use the word *marsupial* and tell about animals with "pockets." Some of these in Australia are kangaroos, koalas, opossums, and wombats.

Kangaroo Babies, and Other Animals and Babies

Materials

- *Does a Kangaroo Have a Mother, Too?* by Eric Carle   • chart paper and marker

Procedure

1. Explain that for human beings, a mother is a *woman*; a father, a *man*; and a young child is called a *baby*. A number of people is called a *group*.

2. Read the book, *Does a Kangaroo Have a Mother, Too?*

3. Make a chart of the names used for baby, parents, and groups of animals. Use the number of animals you feel is appropriate for your class.

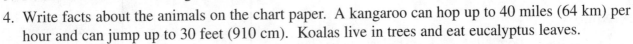

Animal	Baby	Mother	Father	Group
kangaroo	joey	flyer	boomer	troop
lion	cub	lioness	lion	pride
penguin	chick	female	male	colony
swan	cygnet	pen	cob	bevy
fox	cub	vixen	reynard	skulk
dolphin	calf	cow	bull	school
sheep	lamb	ewe	ram	flock
bear	cub	sow	boar	sloth
elephant	calf	cow	bull	herd

Art Activities for Kk

Kite Making

Materials

- *Let's Fly a Kite* by Stuart J. Murphy or *Kites Sail High* by Ruth Heller
- 12" x 18" (30 cm x 46 cm) sheets of construction paper
- scissors
- paper punch
- string
- fabric strips
- double-sided tape
- crayons or markers

Preparation: On each sheet of construction paper, draw a line between the center of the top and bottom (Line 1). Draw another line (Line 2) to guide students when folding down the corners to create the diamond shape.

Procedure

1. Read a book about kites. Ask if students have flown kites.
2. Discuss how much fun it is to fly a kite on a windy day.
3. Fold the paper to create a diamond-shaped kite.
4. Cut out the kite shape.
5. Decorate the kite shape with crayons or markers.
6. Use the paper punch to make a hole at each of the top three points and tie a string through each hole.
7. Tie the strings together in the center of the back and tie one long string around the knot.
8. Tape a strip of fabric to the bottom point and tie a few short strips along the length of the strip.

Kangaroo Mother and Joey

Materials

- kangaroo patterns (page 115)
- scissors
- crayons or markers

Preparation: Duplicate a copy of the kangaroo mother and baby patterns for each child. Cut a slit where the pouch will open.

Procedure

1. Color the kangaroos with crayons or markers
2. Cut out the mother kangaroo and the joey.
3. Put the joey in the pocket and sing the lines to the right to the tune of "London Bridges."

Jumping Joeys

Jumping in and jumping out,
Jumping in, jumping out,
Little joeys jump all day,
In and out.

Kangaroo Mother and Joey

Kangaroo Patterns

Each student will need one copy of this page.

Songs and Fingerplays for Kk

See My Kite

(Sing to the tune of "Twinkle, Twinkle Little Star.")

See my kite fly up so high,
Flying, flying in the sky.
It may reach the clouds one day,
Come with me and we will play.
See my kite fly up so high,
Flying, flying in the sky.

Kookaburra

(Traditional)

Kookaburra sits in the old gum tree.
Merry, merry king of the bush is he.
Laugh, Kookaburra,
Laugh, Kookaburra,
Happy your life must be.

Kookaburra sits in the old gum tree.
Eating all the gumdrops he can see.
Stop, Kookaburra,
Stop, Kookaburra,
Leave some there for me.

Songs and Fingerplays for Kk *(cont.)*

Three Little Kittens

(Traditional)
Three little kittens
They lost their mittens
And they began to cry.
"Oh, Mother, dear, we sadly fear
Our mittens we have lost."

"What! Lost your mittens?
You naughty kittens!
Then you shall have no pie!
Meow, Meow,
Then you shall have no pie!"

The three little kittens
They found their mittens,
And they began to cry,
"Oh, mother, dear, see here, see here,
Our mittens we have found."

"What! Found your mittens?
You good little kittens!
Then you shall have some pie!
Purr-rr, Purr-rr,
Then you shall have some pie!"

My Pocket Book for Kk

Kk

king

1

kite

2

The king flies a kite.

3

Ll

like • lion • look

Story Books

Andy and the Lion by James Daugherty

The Grouchy Ladybug by Eric Carle

The Happy Lion by Louise Fatio

Is Your Mama a Llama? by Deborah Guarino

The Ladybug by Sabrina Crewe

Let's Go Home, Little Bear by Martin Waddell

Look What I Did with a Leaf by Morteza E. Sohi

Lovable Lyle by Bernard Waber

Lyle, Lyle, Crocodile by Bernard Waber

Many Luscious Lollipops by Ruth Heller

Foods/Snacks

- lemon gelatin
- lemon lollipops
- lemonade
- licorice
- limeade

Getting Started

1. Introduce the letter and the special picture. Read a book with the letter **L** in the title. Brainstorm a list of other words that begin with an **Ll** and write the words on a chart. Include the names of any children in the class whose names begin with **L**. (**Note:** When introducing the students to any of the activities or worksheets connected to the letter, the emphasis should be on the connection to the letter and the letter sound.)

2. Play a game of Red Light, Green Light outside or in the gym. Decide the start and finish lines. Choose one student to be "It." The rest of the students stand at the start line. The person who is It stands at the other end of the area. It says, "Green light" and counts to ten with his or her back to the others, while they try to run to the finish line. When It says, "Red light," all the runners must freeze. The teacher stands on the side and sends anyone still moving back to the starting line. It yells, "Green light" again, and the game continues until someone reaches the finish line. The person who reaches the finish line becomes It and the game starts over again.

Language Arts for Ll

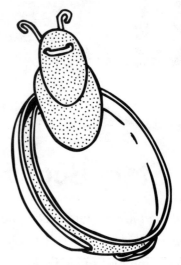

Ladybug Poem

Materials

- chart paper and marker
- paper plates (two per child)
- red and black paint
- paintbrushes
- scissors
- glue
- paper punch
- sheets of black construction paper (one per child)
- yellow paper
- chenille sticks (one per child)

Preparation: Cut two black ovals, one larger than the other, from each sheet of black paper. These are for the ladybug's head and abdomen. Cut six legs from the black paper for each ladybug. Cut out many small circles from the yellow paper. On chart paper, write the following poem:

Ladybug

Ladybug, ladybug,
Fly away home,
Your house is on fire
And your children are gone.

Procedure

1. Read the poem and discuss it.
2. Have each student paint the underside of one paper plate black and one paper plate red. Let dry.
3. Cut a narrow triangle out of the red plate to make wings and glue on top of the black plate.
4. Paste the oval for the thorax on the oval for the head. Attatch them to the plate to make three body parts.
5. Use the paper punch to make two holes in the head and put a short chenille stick through for antennae.
6. Glue yellow spots on the wings.
7. Reread the poem and brainstorm other reasons why the ladybug would want to go home. Write the new ideas on the chart. Read the new poems and illustrate them. For example:

Ladybug Poems

Ladybug, ladybug,
Fly away home,
It is time for lunch
And your soup's getting cold.

Ladybug, ladybug,
Fly away home,
Your mother is calling
And she's looking for you.

Name _____

Printing Practice for Ll

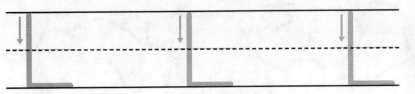

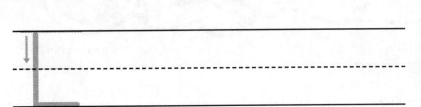

lion

Name _____

Word Practice for Ll

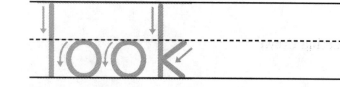
lion

look

like

We look at lions.

Science Activities for Ll

Learn About Leaves

Read a nonfiction book about leaves. Make leaf rubbings and display the leaves with the rubbings.

Materials

- *Tell Me, Tree* by Gail Gibbons or *Look What I Did with a Leaf* by Morteza E. Sohi
- leaves
- thin copy paper
- crayons with paper removed
- chart paper and marker

Procedure

1. Show a leaf. Ask students what they already know about leaves and write answers on a word map.
2. Read a book to the class about trees and leaves. Add new ideas to the word map.
3. Put a leaf under the paper and use the side of a crayon to rub over the leaf.
4. Display the leaves, the rubbings, and the word map.

Learn About Ladybugs

Materials

- *Ladybug* by Karen Hartley or *The Ladybug* by Sabrina Crewe
- paper for each child
- crayons or markers
- book binding materials (stapler, rings, etc.)

Procedure

1. Show a picture of a ladybug and recite "Ladybug Poem" (page 120).
2. Read a nonfiction book about ladybugs.
3. Ask students to recall facts about ladybugs and write each fact at the bottom of a sheet of paper. If preferred, pages with a sentence printed at the bottom can be prepared ahead of time on your computer. Some suggested sentences:

- Ladybugs are insects.
- Ladybugs have six legs.
- Ladybugs can fly.
- Ladybugs have spots.
- Ladybugs eat aphids.
- Ladybugs lay eggs.
- Ladybugs are small beetles.
- Ladybugs have two pairs of wings.
- Ladybugs have two eyes.
- Ladybugs have two antennae.

4. Illustrate each page and put the pages together to create a class book.

Art Activities for Ll

Lion Paintings

Materials

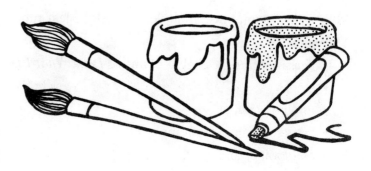

- orange and yellow paint
- paintbrushes
- round sponges
- black marker
- large sheets of white paper (one per child)
- large sheet of chart paper or butcher paper
- newspaper

Procedure

1. Using a large sheet of paper, demonstrate painting a lion. Using yellow paint, paint a circle for the head, two small circles for ears, a rectangle with rounded corners for the body, four legs, and a long tail with a brush at the end.

2. Let this dry, and then paint the mane. Make circles around the head using orange paint and brushes or sponges.

3. When the mane is dry, add face, whiskers, and claws with a black marker.

4. Distribute paper and yellow paint to the students to paint the heads, bodies, legs, and tails.

5. Let the paintings dry, and then paint the orange manes.

6. Add details with the black markers.

7. Display the lion paintings with the title, "We Like to Look at Lions."

Art Activities for Ll *(cont.)*

Lemon Lollipop Prints

Materials

- lemons
- sharp knife for teacher use
- sheets of white or colored paper (one per child)
- yellow paint
- glue
- scissors
- craft sticks
- paintbrushes
- paper plates (optional)

Preparation: Cut lemons in half and let it dry for an hour or more so the segments will stand out.

Procedure

1. Using the paintbrush, paint the cut half of the lemon with yellow paint. Or, dip the lemon in paint poured on a plate.
2. Make three or four prints of the lemon on the paper. Try to spread them apart. Cut out the prints when they are dry.
3. Put glue on craft sticks and add them to the picture to look like lollipops.
4. Display them with the title, "Lovely Lemon Lollipops."

Leaf-People Pictures

Materials

- leaves from different trees
- glue
- paper
- crayons or markers

Preparation: Flatten the leaves by placing them beneath a pile of books for a day.

Procedure

1. Put glue on the backs of the leaves.
2. Put the leaf in the center of the paper, with the glued side down.
3. Using crayons or markers, add a head, arms, and legs.
4. Decorate the rest of the paper to create a scene.
5. Display the pictures with the title, "Leaf-People Pictures."

Songs and Fingerplays for Ll

London Bridge

(Traditional)

London Bridge is falling down,
Falling down, falling down,
London Bridge is falling down,
My fair lady!
Take a key and lock her up,
Lock her up, lock her up,
Take a key and lock her up.
My fair lady!

Leaf Song

(Sing to the tune of "Twinkle, Twinkle, Little Star.")

Leaves are falling, down, down, down
Leaves are falling to the ground.
Red and yellow, orange ones, too
I can see them, so can you,
Leaves are falling, down, down, down
Leaves are falling to the ground.

Did You Ever See a Lion?

(Sing to the tune of "Did You Ever See a Lassie?")

Did you ever hear a lion, a lion, a lion,
Did you ever hear a lion, give a loud roar?
A loud roar, a loud roar, a loud roar, a loud roar,
Did you ever hear a lion, give a loud roar?
(Roar!)

Did you ever see a lion, a lion, a lion,
Did you ever see a lion, turn right around?
Turn around, and turn around,
And turn around, and turn around,
Did you ever see a lion, turn right around?
(Turn around.)

My Pocket Book for Ll

Ll

look   1

lion   2

I like to look at the lion.   3

Mm

mom • mouse • my

Story Books

Caps for Sale by Esphyr Slobodkina
Goodnight Moon by Margaret Wise Brown
If You Give a Moose a Muffin
   by Laura Joffe Numeroff
If You Give a Mouse a Cookie
   by Laura Joffe Numeroff
Mike Mulligan and His Steam Shovel
   by Virginia Lee Burton
The Moon Book by Gail Gibbons
Moongame by Frank Asch
"More, More, More," Said the Baby
   by Vera B. Williams
No Jumping on the Bed! by Tedd Arnold
Science with Magnets by Helen Edom

Foods/Snacks

- macaroni
- marshmallows
- milk
- milkshakes
- mints
- muffins

Getting Started

1. Introduce the letter and the special picture. Read a book with the letter **M** in the title. Brainstorm a list of other words that begin with an **Mm** and write the words on a chart. Include the names of any children in the class whose names begin with **M**. (**Note:** When introducing the students to any of the activities or worksheets connected to the letter, the emphasis should be on the connection to the letter and the letter sound.)

2. Dramatize "The Muffin Man" song. Have the students stand in a circle. Sing the first verse while one student walks around the inside of the circle. He or she will stop in front of one student, and all will sing the second verse. Then the two students will walk together.

The Muffin Man

Oh, do you know the muffin man,
The muffin man, the muffin man?
Oh, do you know the muffin man,
Who lives on Drury Lane?

Oh, yes I know the muffin man,
The muffin man, the muffin man.
Oh, yes I know the muffin man,
Who lives on Drury Lane.

Language Arts for Mm

Me Books

Materials

- 12" x 18" (30 x 46 cm) sheets of construction paper (4 per student)
- comb binding or ring binders
- crayons or markers
- glue
- scissors
- sentences (page 130)

Preparation: Cut each sheet of construction paper into three parts, each 6" x 12" (15 cm x 30 cm). Put the books together using 11 of these sheets. Bind the books using comb binding or ring binders. Duplicate the sentences for each student. Cut out and glue the title of the book at the top of the first page.

Procedure

1. Have each child draw a picture of himself or herself on the cover, under the title.

2. Discuss what might be drawn on the second page and have students glue the second line at the bottom of the second page and draw pictures.

3. Repeat the process until the book is complete.

Miss Muffet

Materials

- chair or small stool
- toy spider or paper spider
- bowl and spoon

Procedure

1. Choose a girl to sit on the chair and hold the bowl and spoon.

2. Another student will hold the spider.

3. Recite the nursery rhyme while it is being acted out.

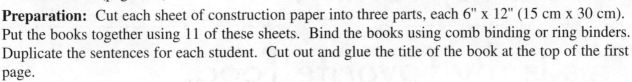

Little Miss Muffet

Little Miss Muffet sat on a tuffet
Eating her curds and whey.
Along came a spider
who sat down beside her
And frightened Miss Muffet away.

Me Books

All About Me

This is my house.

Here is my family.

This is my favorite food.

This is my favorite toy.

This is my school.

Here is my friend.

This is my favorite book.

This is my teacher.

This is my favorite place to visit.

The End

Name _____

Printing Practice for Mm

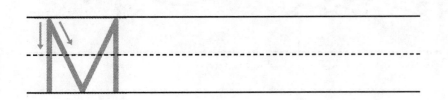

mouse

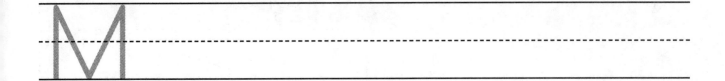

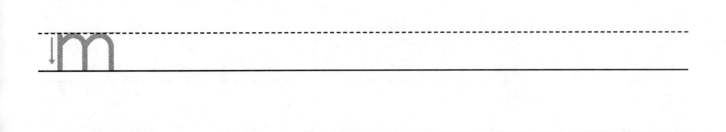

Name _____

Word Practice for Mm

mouse

mom

my

Mom saw the moon.

Science Activities for Mm

Magnets

Learn about the things a magnet will and will not attract.

Materials

- *Science with Magnets* by Helen Edom
- magnets (one per group of students)
- bags of a variety of objects (one per group of students)
- chart paper and marker
- sheets of paper (one per group)

Preparation: Fold the sheets of paper in half and write "Will Attract" on one side and "Will Not Attract" on the other side.

Procedure

1. Make predictions about what will happen to each of several objects when it gets near a magnet.
2. Write the students' predictions on chart paper.
3. Read and discuss the book, *Science with Magnets*.
4. Distribute a magnet and bag of objects to each group.
5. Encourage students to test each item with the magnet.
6. Sort the objects, and place each one on the paper on the correct side.
7. Confirm predictions and write conclusions on the chart.

Moon

Learn facts about the moon. Have the students watch for a full moon in the evenings.

Materials

- *The Moon Book* by Gail Gibbons
- chart paper and marker
- 12" x 18" (30 cm x 46 cm) sheets of dark blue or black construction paper (one per child)
- scissors
- white, yellow, and gray paint in shallow dishes
- sponges
- newspaper
- cardboard
- picture of a full moon

Preparation: Cut a 10" (25 cm) round hole from cardboard to create a moon template. Pour the paint into shallow dishes.

Procedure

1. Show a picture of a full moon. Ask students what they already know about the moon and write their responses on the chart.
2. Read a nonfiction book about the moon. Add additional facts about the moon to the chart after reading the book.
3. Place a sheet of dark construction paper on newspaper, put the moon template on the paper.
4. Dip the sponge in the white paint first, and dab the sponge all over the inside of the circle.
5. Add a few dabs of yellow and gray paint.
6. When dry, display the moon pictures with the chart and the title, "Many Moons."

Art Activities for Mm

Marble Paintings

Materials

- empty gift boxes or plastic tubs (one per child)
- marbles
- plastic cups
- red, orange, yellow, green, blue, and purple paint
- plastic spoons
- newspaper

Preparation: Pour a small amount of paint into each cup. (The paint may need to be watered down a bit.) Spread newspaper out on the floor and tables in the activity area.

Procedure

1. Add a few marbles to the paint.
2. Use a spoon to pick up the marble and put it in the box. Put the spoon back in the same color.
3. Tilt the box in various directions until most of the paint is off the marble.
4. Use the spoon to put the marble back in the correct paint color.
5. Repeat the process using different colors.
6. Display with the title, "Marble Paintings."
   (**Optional:** Use a larger box and have one child hold each end.)

Monkeys and Caps

Materials

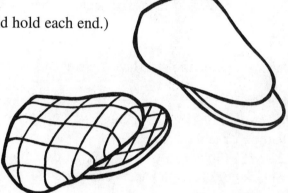

- *Caps for Sale* by Esphyr Slobodkina
- sheets of white cardstock (two per child)
- monkey and cap patterns (pages 135–136)
- crayons or markers
- large sheet of brown paper
- scissors
- tape

Preparation: Draw a large tree with many branches on the brown paper. Duplicate the monkey and cap patterns onto white cardstock for each child.

Procedure

1. Read the book, *Caps for Sale*.
2. Color the monkeys.
3. Color the caps according to the colors (red, blue, gray, brown, and one checked cap) in the book.
4. Cut out the monkeys and the caps. Put a piece of tape on each monkey and each cap.
5. Hang up the tree.
6. Choose a student to be the peddler and have him hold the checked cap on his head with all the caps stacked on top in order.
7. Reread the book, and act out the story, having students tape the monkeys to the tree and putting a hat on each monkey at the appropriate time. Put the book, the monkeys, the tape, and the hats in the reading center.

Monkeys and Caps

Monkey Pattern

Use these to dramatize *Caps for Sale* by Esphyr Slobodkina.
Each student will need one copy of this page on white cardstock.

Monkeys and Caps *(cont.)*

Cap Patterns

Use these to dramatize *Caps for Sale* by Esphyr Slobodkina. Each student will need one copy of this page.

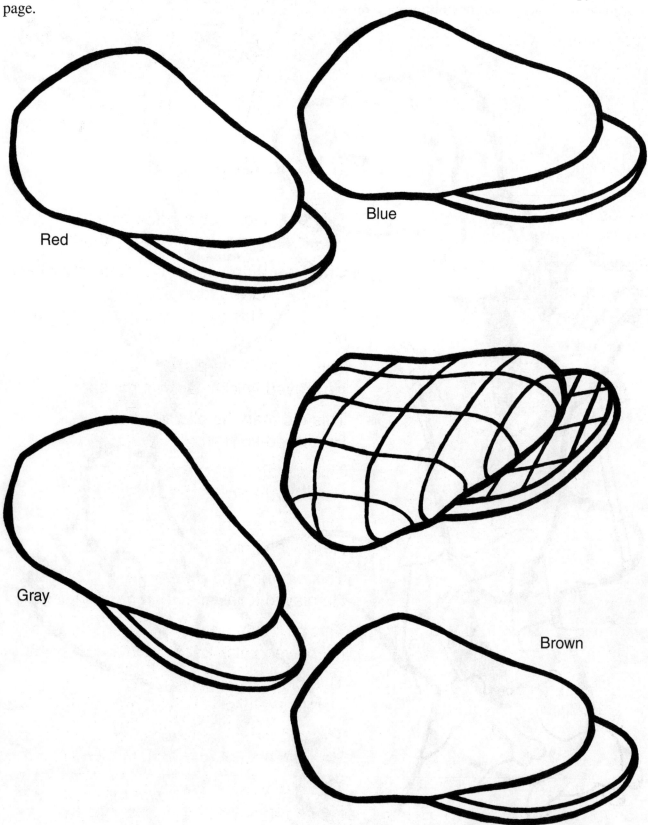

Songs and Fingerplays for Mm

Once There Were Two Monkeys

Once there were two monkeys
Who did not get along.
Every time they argued
They used to sing this song:
Stand up, sit down,
That's the way it goes
Stand up, sit down
Finger on your nose.

(Repeat using the following phrases.)

Hands up, hands down
Foot up, foot down
Elbows up, elbows down
Eyes up, eyes down
Face up, face down

This Old Man

(Traditional)
This old man, he played one
He played knick-knack on my thumb.

Chorus: With a knick-knack paddy whack
 Give a dog a bone,
 This old man came rolling home.

(Repeat chorus after each two-line verse).

This old man, he played two
He played knick-knack on my shoe.

This old man, he played three
He played knick-knack on my knee.

This old man, he played four
He played knick-knack on my door.

This old man, he played five
He played knick-knack on my side.

This old man, he played six
He played knick-knack on my sticks

This old man, he played seven
He played knick-knack up in heaven.

This old man, he played eight
He played knick-knack at my gate.

This old man, he played nine
He played knick-knack all the time.

This old man, he played ten
He played knick-knack over again.

My Pocket Book for Mm

M m

mouse

1

moon

2

My mouse sees the moon.

3

138

Nn

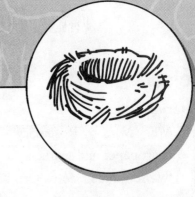

nest • no • not

Story Books

The Best Nest by P. D. Eastman
A Nest Full of Eggs by Priscilla Belz Jenkins
A New Coat for Anna by Harriet Ziefert
No Jumping on the Bed! by Ted Arnold
Noisy Nora by Rosemary Wells
The Nose Book by Al Perkins
Nuts to You! by Lois Ehlert
There's a Nightmare in My Closet by Mercer Mayer
The Very Noisy Night by Diana Hendry
What Makes Day and Night? by Franklyn M. Branley

Foods/Snacks

- nachos
- nectarines
- noodle soup
- noodles
- nuts

Getting Started

1. Introduce the letter and the special picture. Read a book with the letter **N** in the title. Brainstorm a list of other words that begin with an **Nn** and write the words on a chart. Include the names of any children in the class whose names begin with **N**. (**Note:** When introducing the students to any of the activities or worksheets connected to the letter, the emphasis should be on the connection to the letter and the letter sound.)

2. Read the book, *Nuts to You*, about the playful activities of a squirrel. Talk about the methods squirrels use to find and store nuts. Dramatize finding and storing nuts. Teach the students the game, Squirrel in the Tree. Have pairs of students form a "tree" by holding both hands. Choose students to be "squirrels." There has to be at least one more squirrel than there are trees. When the teacher calls, "Squirrels change," the squirrels must run to a new tree. Squirrels who do not find a tree have to wait until the teacher calls for squirrels to change trees again. Change the squirrels and trees until everyone has had an opportunity to be in both positions.

Language Arts for Nn

Noise

Materials

- *Noisy Nora* by Rosemary Wells and *The Very Noisy Night* by Diana Hendry
- chart paper and marker
- two felt mice (see pattern below)
- tiny quilt
- feltboard
- kitchen utensils
- marching music tape or CD
- "Noisy Nora" song (page 146)

Procedure

1. Show kitchen utensils and make noise with some of them.
2. Discuss noise. What makes noise?
3. Develop a word map of the students' responses.
4. Show the cover of *Noisy Nora* and make predictions about what Nora might do to make noise, and why she is making so much noise.
5. Read the book.
6. Sing the song, "Noisy Nora"
7. Read *The Very Noisy Night*. Use the felt mice and the quilt to tell the story on the feltboard.

Mouse Patterns

Name _____

Printing Practice for Nn

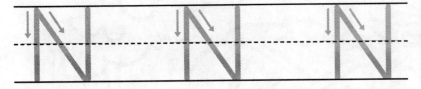

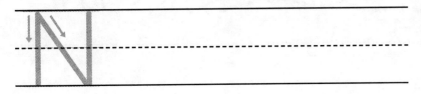

nest

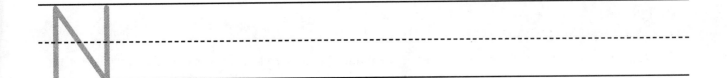

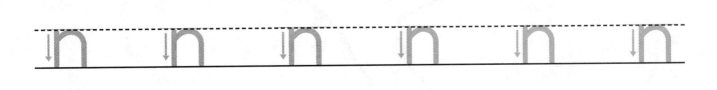

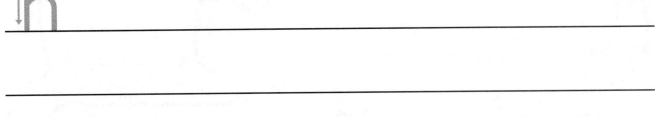

Word Practice for Nn

nest

no

not

I see a nest.

Science Activities for Nn

Nests

Read a nonfiction book about nests. Discuss different kinds of nests made by different birds.

Materials
- *A Nest Full of Eggs* by Priscilla Belz Jenkins or *The Best Nest* by P. D. Eastman
- coffee filters (round, not cone shaped)
- craft sticks
- cellophane grass, raffia, or straw
- glue
- modeling clay or craft dough
- paint
- sentence practice sheets
- paintbrushes

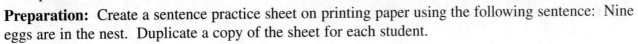

Preparation: Create a sentence practice sheet on printing paper using the following sentence: Nine eggs are in the nest. Duplicate a copy of the sheet for each student.

Procedure
1. Read a book about nests. Point out several types of nests and how birds use different materials to build their nests.
2. Make eggs from modeling clay and let them dry.
3. Paint the eggs and set them aside to dry.
4. Use craft sticks to spread glue on the coffee filters.
5. Cover the glue with cellophane grass.
6. Put the eggs in the nests and display with the completed sentence practice sheets.

Night and Day

Learn about what makes day and night.

Materials
- *What Makes Day and Night?* by Franklyn M. Branley
- globe
- flashlight
- chart paper and marker
- paper flag

Procedure
1. Read a nonfiction book about the differences between night and day.
2. Place the globe on a table in the center of the room.
3. Put a little paper flag on the globe to mark your location.
4. Darken the room, and turn the globe slowly. Shine the flashlight on the globe to represent the sun. The beam of light stays stationary while the globe is turned. Keep track of the flag as the light changes.
5. Discuss why we do some things at night and some things during the day.
6. Write "Day" on one side of the chart and "Night" on the other side. Brainstorm things that happen at night and during the day.

Art Activities for Nn

Nocturnal Animals

Materials

- nocturnal animal patterns (page 145)
- tin foil circles (one per child)
- chart paper and marker
- crayons
- scissors
- glue
- 9" x 12" (23 cm x 30 cm) sheets of white construction paper
- black paint
- wide paintbrushes

Preparation: Duplicate the nocturnal animal patterns for each child. Thin the paint with water.

Procedure

1. Distribute the patterns of nocturnal animals.
2. Tell the students that animals that are awake at night and sleep during the day are called "nocturnal."
3. Write "Nocturnal Animals" at the top of the chart, and then write the names of some of the animals.
4. Using wax crayons, color the animals, pressing down hard on the crayons.
5. Cut out the animals. Glue the animals and the tin foil moon on the white construction paper. Using crayons, draw a few rocks and trees.
6. To create a night sky, use the wide paintbrush, dip it in the black paint, and draw the brush over the whole paper once. The paint should bead up on the wax from the crayons.
7. Display the pictures with the chart.

Note Paper

Materials

- copy paper
- envelopes
- markers
- pencils
- rubber stamps
- ink pads

Procedure

1. Discuss writing notes and how nice it is to receive them.
2. Use rubber stamps to decorate around the edge of the paper. On the center of the paper, write a message or draw a picture.
3. Fold the note and put it in the envelope.
4. Give the note to someone special.

Nocturnal Animals

Nocturnal Animal Patterns

Each student will need one copy of this page.

1. raccoon
2. owl
3. firefly
4. hedgehog
5. skunk
6. bat

Songs and Fingerplays for Nn

Noisy Nora

(Sing to the tune of "Twinkle, Twinkle Little Star.")

Noisy Nora, come and play,

We can have fun all the day.

We can work and we can play,

"This is fun," you will say,

Noisy Nora, come and play,

We can have fun all the day.

Nine More Miles

(Traditional)

Nine more miles,

Nine more miles

(Hold up nine fingers.)

Nine more miles to go-o

Pick up your feet

(Raise knees.)

And swing your arms

(Swing arms.)

Nine more miles to go.

(Continue with the following verses using the correct actions.)

Eight more miles,

Seven more miles,

Six more miles,

Five more miles,

Four more miles,

Three more miles,

Two more miles,

One more mile,

No more miles,

Variations: Sit down to sing or sing very slowly.

Songs and Fingerplays for Nn *(cont.)*

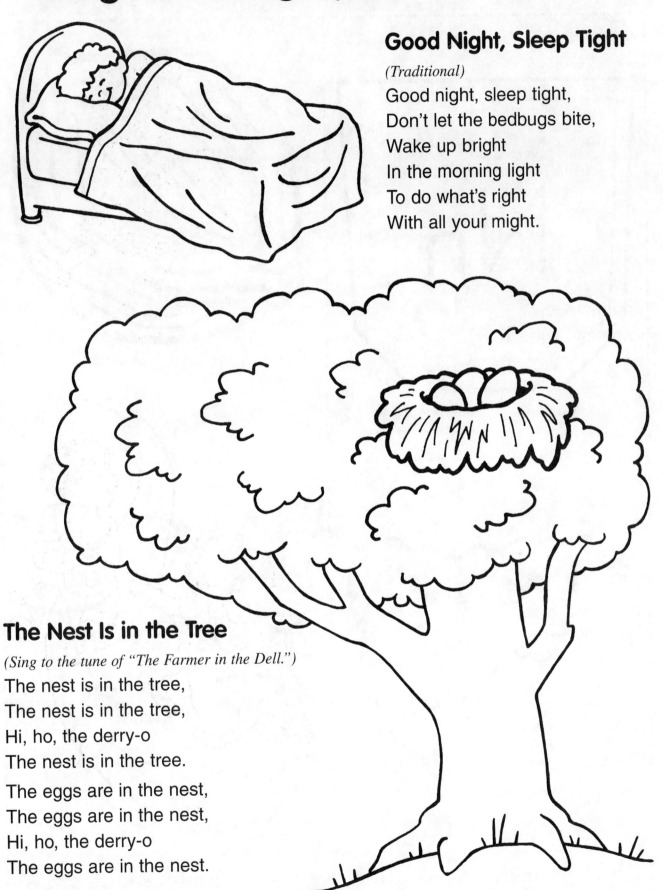

Good Night, Sleep Tight

(Traditional)
Good night, sleep tight,
Don't let the bedbugs bite,
Wake up bright
In the morning light
To do what's right
With all your might.

The Nest Is in the Tree

(Sing to the tune of "The Farmer in the Dell.")
The nest is in the tree,
The nest is in the tree,
Hi, ho, the derry-o
The nest is in the tree.

The eggs are in the nest,
The eggs are in the nest,
Hi, ho, the derry-o
The eggs are in the nest.

My Pocket Book for Nn

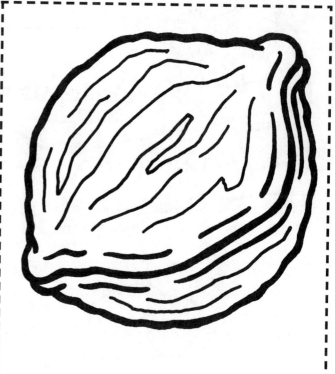

nut

1

nest

2

A nut is in the nest.

3

octopus • on • our

Story Books

A Fish Out of Water by Helen Palmer
My Very Own Octopus by Bernard Most
An Octopus Is Amazing by Patricia Lauber
Octopus Under the Sea by Connie and Peter Roop
Officer Buckle and Gloria by Peggy Rathmann
Oliver by Syd Hoff
Opossum at Sycamore Road by Sally M. Walker
Opposites by Sandra Boynton
Oscar Otter by Nathaniel Benchley
Welcome to the World of Octopus by Diane Swanson

Foods/Snacks

- olives
- omelets
- O-shaped cereal
- pretzel rings

Getting Started

1. Introduce the letter and the special picture. Read a book with the letter **O** in the title. Brainstorm a list of other words that begin with an **Oo** and write the words on a chart. Include the names of any children in the class whose names begin with **O**. (**Note:** When introducing the students to any of the activities or worksheets connected to the letter, the emphasis should be on the connection to the letter and the letter sound.)

2. Play with large hoops. Call them "giant O's." Use hoops in the gym or out of doors. You will need a hoop for each one or two students. Follow the directions below or use your own ideas to make the connection between the shape of the hoop and the letter **Oo**.

   - put the hoop on the ground and walk around it
   - jump in and out of the hoop
   - step in and out of the hoop
   - hop in and out of the hoop
   - run around the hoop
   - step inside and lift the hoop over your head
   - put the hoop on your hips and try to keep it up by rolling your hips around

Language Arts for Oo

Opposites

Materials

- *Opposites* by Sandra Boynton
- chart paper and marker
- sentence strips
- pencils
- 12" x 18" (30 cm x 46 cm) sheets of paper
- scissors
- crayons or markers

Preparation: Fold each sheet of paper in half.

Procedure

1. Write the word "Opposites" at the top of the chart.
2. Make two columns on the chart.
3. Discuss the idea of opposites by giving a few examples: *hot/cold, in/out, fast/slow, over/under, up/down, on/off.*
4. Read the book, *Opposites*. Note the opposites mentioned.
5. Brainstorm a list of opposites and add to the chart until there are enough examples for each student, or each pair of students.
6. Distribute copies of the sentence strip below and print the words for opposites on the lines.

7. Cut the strips out on the lines.
8. Paste the beginning part of the sentence strip at the top of the left side of the construction paper and the end of the sentence at the top of the right side.
9. Draw a picture for each side of the paper that illustrates the opposites.
10. Put the pages together to create a class Big Book of Opposites.
11. Make a cover and title the book, "Oscar's Opposites."

Oscar thought it was _____,

but it was _____.

Name _____

Printing Practice for Oo

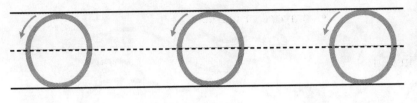

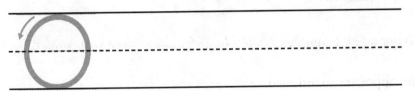

octopus

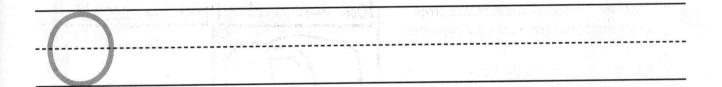

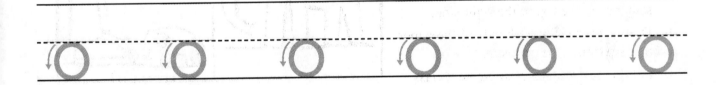

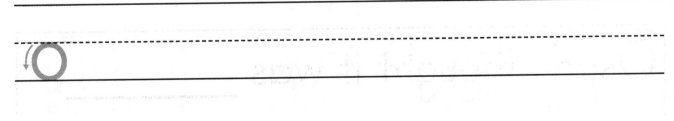

Word Practice for Oo

octopus

on

our

I have an octopus.

Science Activities for Oo

Octopus

Read a nonfiction book about an octopus. Make an octopus puppet and sing an octopus song.

Materials

- *An Octopus Is Amazing* by Patricia Lauber, *Octopus Under the Sea* by Connie and Peter Roop
- chart paper and marker
- 6" x 9" (15 cm x 23 cm) felt rectangles (red, orange, yellow, green, gray, blue, or purple)
- large wiggle eyes
- glue
- black permanent markers
- scissors

Procedure

1. Read a book about an octopus.
2. Write "Octopus" at the top of the chart, then help students recall facts about an octopus and write them on the chart. Some examples are listed here:

    - An octopus lives in water.
    - An octopus has eight tentacles or legs.
    - An octopus has no bones.
    - An octopus has two big eyes.

    - An octopus can change its color.
    - An octopus lives in a cave in rocks.
    - An octopus lays hundreds of eggs.

3. Prepare octopus puppets. For each puppet, cut off the top corners of two of the felt rectangles to create a rounded edge. Cut three slits half way up from the bottom of each rectangle to form eight legs.
4. Glue or sew around the top half to form puppets.
5. Glue wiggle eyes in place.
6. Use markers to draw circles on the legs for suckers.
7. With puppets on hands, stand and sing "The Octopus Song" (page 156).

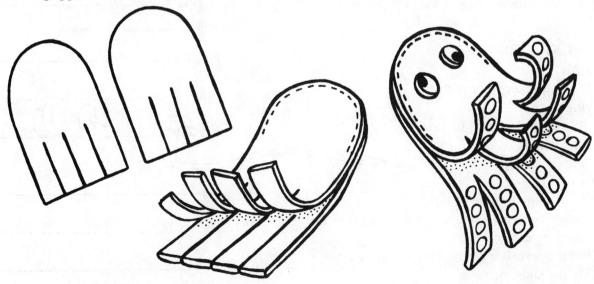

Art Activities for Oo

Octopus Mural

Make a mural of an octopus habitat.

Materials
- mural paper
- blue, green, gray, and brown paint
- large paintbrushes
- octopus patterns (page 155)
- crayons or markers
- scissors
- glue
- newspaper
- green tissue paper (optional)

Preparation: Thin the blue paint with water. Duplicate the octopus patterns for each student. Put mural paper on the floor on plenty of newspaper.

Procedure
1. Paint the paper with the blue paint thinned with water to look like water.
2. When dry, use gray and brown paint to make rocks at the bottom of the paper.
3. Use green paint to make seaweed. For added texture, add strips of green crumpled tissue to the wet paint for more seaweed.
4. Color the octopus patterns.
5. Cut out the animals and glue them on the mural.
6. Display the mural with the chart about the octopus developed in the science activity.

O Pictures

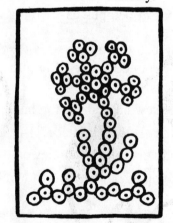

Materials
- O–shaped cereal in small plastic cups (one per child)
- 6" x 9" (15 cm x 23 cm) sheets of construction paper
- glue

Preparation: Put the cereal in small cups.

Procedure
1. Design pictures on the paper and glue the cereal in place.
2. Display with the title, "Our **O** Pictures."

O Necklaces

Materials
- O–shaped cereal or pretzel rings
- 30" (81 cm) lengths of string (one per child)
- cellophane tape

Procedure
1. Wrap a small piece of tape around one end of the string and a knot in the other end. This will create a "needle" to make stringing easier.
2. Put the cereal or pretzels on the string.
3. Tie the ends together.

Octopus Mural

Octopus Patterns

Each student will need one copy of this page.

Songs and Fingerplays for Oo

The Octopus Song

(Sing to the tune of "Mary Had a Little Lamb.")

The octopus is swimming by,
Swimming by
Swimming by
The octopus is swimming by,
It can swim so fast.

The octopus has eight big legs,
Eight big legs
Eight big legs
The octopus has eight big legs
The legs can catch some food.

The octopus has no bones,
Has no bones
Has no bones
The octopus has no bones,
It can change its shape.

The octopus has two big eyes,
Two big eyes
Two big eyes
The octopus has two big eyes,
To help it look for food.

The octopus can change its color
Change its color,
Change its color,
The octopus can change its color,
It helps to keep it safe.

The octopus lives in the rocks,
In the rocks
In the rocks
The octopus lives in the rocks,
It can hide all day.

The octopus lays hundreds of eggs,
Hundreds of eggs
Hundreds of eggs
The octopus lays hundreds of eggs,
They hatch and swim away.

Songs and Fingerplays for Oo *(cont.)*

Oh, Dear, What Can The Matter Be?

(Traditional)
Oh, dear, what can the matter be?
Oh, dear, what can the matter be?
Oh, dear, what can the matter be
Johnny's so long at the fair.

Oh, he promised to buy me some bonnie blue ribbons,
He promised to buy me some bonnie blue ribbons,
He promised to buy me some bonnie blue ribbons,
To tie up my bonnie brown hair.

Oh, dear, what can the matter be?
Oh, dear, what can the matter be?
Oh, dear, what can the matter be
Johnny's so long at the fair.

Otter Song

(Sing to the tune of "Here We Go Round the Mulberry Bush.")

Sea otter swims out in the sea,
in the sea, in the sea.
Sea otter swims out in the sea, fast as he can be.

He swims through kelp and dives for food,
dives for food, dives for food
He swims through kelp and dives for food, fast as he can be.

He breaks shells open on a rock,
on a rock, on a rock.
He breaks shells open on a rock, so he can eat the food.

When he rests he floats on his back,
floats on his back, floats on his back.
When he rests he floats on his back, oh, so quietly.

My Pocket Book for Oo

octopus 1

on 2

The octopus is on the rock. 3

Pp

pen • pig • play

Story Books

Harold and the Purple Crayon by Crockett Johnson
If You Give a Pig a Pancake by Laura Numeroff
Panda Bear, Panda Bear, What Do You See?
   by Bill Martin Jr.
Penguin Pete by Marcus Pfister
Penguins by Gail Gibbons
Pigs by Gail Gibbons
Polar Bear, Polar Bear, What Do You Hear?
   by Bill Martin Jr.
The Popcorn Book by Tomie dePaola
Pumpkin Day, Pumpkin Night by Anne Rockwell
Three Little Pigs by Paul Galdone

Foods/Snacks

- pancakes
- peanut butter
- peanuts
- pizza
- pop (soda)
- popcorn
- popsicles
- pretzels
- pumpkin pie

Getting Started

1. Introduce the letter and the special picture. Read a book with the letter **P** in the title. Brainstorm a list of other words that begin with a **Pp** and write the words on a chart. Include the names of any children in the class whose names begin with **P**. (**Note:** When introducing the students to any of the activities or worksheets connected to the letter, the emphasis should be on the connection to the letter and the letter sound.)

2. Make pompoms from 10 strips, 12" (30 cm) of purple (or your school colors) crepe paper rolled together at one end and wrapped with masking tape. Each student will need two pompoms. Line up as cheerleaders in the gym or outside. The leader will yell, "Give me a **P**!" Students yell, "**P**!" "Give me an **O**!"
Repeat until students have spelled the word "pompom." Then yell, "What do you have?" Students yell, "Pompom!" This can be repeated using the special words that begin with the letter **Pp**: pig, play, and pen.

Language Arts for Pp

Pancakes

Have a pancake party and read books about pancakes.

Materials

- *If You Give a Pig a Pancake* by Laura Numeroff or *Pancakes, Pancakes!* by Eric Carle
- ingredients for pancakes (see Preparation section)
- electric frying pan
- cooking spray
- bowl
- wire whisk
- spoon
- syrup, in a squeeze bottle
- paper plates (one per child)
- napkins (one per child)
- forks (one per child)
- chart paper and marker
- camera

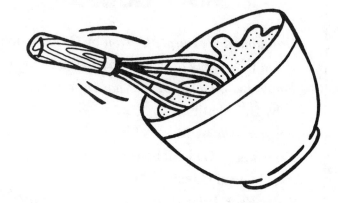

Preparation: Gather the following ingredients: 2 eggs, 2 cups (450 g) flour, 1½ cups (360 mL) milk, ¼ cup (60 mL) vegetable oil, 2 tablespoons (30 mL) sugar, 2 tablespoons (30 mL) baking powder, and 1 teaspoon (5 mL) salt.

Procedure

1. Brainstorm what would happen if you gave a pig a pancake, then read *If You Give a Pig a Pancake*.

2. Start heating the frying pan. Spray with cooking spray.

3. Beat the eggs with a wire whisk and add the other ingredients. Whisk until fairly smooth.

4. Drop by spoonfuls onto the hot pan. Cook one side of the pancake and flip it over to cook the other side.

5. Serve pancakes with syrup.

6. Take photos during this procedure. (**Management Tip:** It takes quite a bit of time to cook pancakes for a group. Parents or volunteers with extra frying pans would mean that more students could be served at one time. Or, prepare pancakes ahead of time and keep them warm.)

7. Read *Pancakes, Pancakes!* by Eric Carle.

8. Write the words, "Pancakes, Pancakes" at the top of the chart. Brainstorm words that could be used to describe the pancakes (*perfect, plump*) and write them on the chart.

9. When the photos are developed, add the pictures to the chart.

Name _____

Printing Practice for Pp

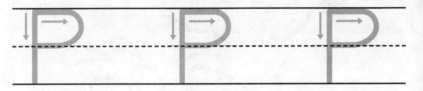

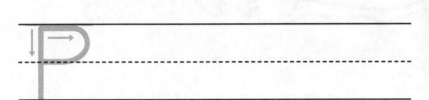

pig

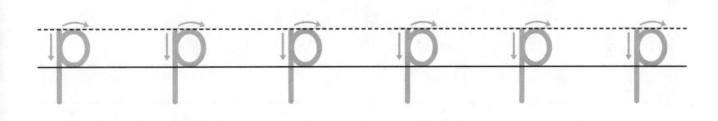

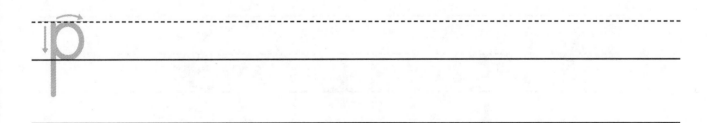

Name _____

Word Practice for Pp

pig

play

pen

The pig plays.

Science Activities for Pp

Penguins

Materials

- *Penguins!* by Gail Gibbons, *The Penguin (Animal Close-Ups)* by Beatrice Fontanel, et al. or *These Birds Can't Fly* by Allan Fowler
- chart paper and marker
- black, white, and yellow paint
- paintbrushes
- sheets of white construction paper (one per child)
- scissors

Procedure

1. Read a nonfiction book about penguins.
2. Write facts about penguins on the chart.
3. Paint penguins by starting with black paint and painting a large oval shape. Paint a head and feet.
4. When this is dry, use the white paint to add an oval on the chest and the eyes. Use the yellow paint for the bill.
5. Cut the chart apart into sentence strips.
6. Display sentence strips with the paintings of penguins.
7. Put the title on the display, "Painted Penguins."
8. For fun, read the story book, *Penguin Pete* by Marcus Pfister.

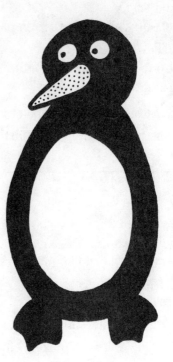

Pandas

Materials

- *The Giant Panda* by Carol A. Amato or *Giant Pandas* by Gail Gibbons
- white paper plates (one per child)
- 2" (5 cm) diameter black circles (four per child)
- blank sentence strips
- black markers
- glue

Procedure

1. Read a book about pandas.
2. Write the facts about pandas on the sentence strips.
3. Make panda faces. Use the black circles for eyes and ears. Glue them onto the paper plate.
4. Using the marker, draw a wide, rounded **V** for the nose and a smile for a mouth.
5. Reread the sentences on the strips.
6. Display the sentences with the panda faces.

Art Activities for Pp

Pink and Purple Polka Dot Pictures

Materials
- pink and purple paint
- plastic bowls
- cotton swabs
- sheets of white construction paper (one per child)
- newspaper

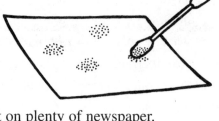

Preparation: Pour the paint in the bowls. Put the bowls of paint on plenty of newspaper.

Procedure

1. Dip cotton swabs in the paint and put dots on the paper.
2. Let the pictures dry and display with the title, "Pink and Purple Polka Dot Pictures."

Potato Prints

Materials
- paint
- paintbrushes
- 4 potatoes, cut in half
- paper

Procedure

1. Paint the flat side of the potatoes with paint and print on the paper.
2. Use many colors to make a capital **P**.
3. Display with the title, "Potato Print **P**'s."

Pink Pop-up Pigs

Materials
- pop-up pig pattern (page 165)
- sheets of pink construction paper (one per child)
- pink paper ovals (one per child)
- pink paper triangles (two per child)
- scissors
- glue
- black markers

Preparation: Duplicate the pop-up pig pattern onto pink construction paper for each child.

Procedure

1. Distribute copies of the pig and fold on the dashed line. Make certain the illustration is on the outside.
2. While the paper is folded, cut around the **P** (solid lines).
3. Go over the line between the legs and color the toes with the black marker.
4. Lay the paper down with the folded edge toward you, and then fold the pig up. Paste the pink oval on the **P** for the nose and the triangles for ears. Open the sheet and pop the pig to the other side. Display the pop-up pigs on a table.

Pink Pop-up Pigs

Pop-up Pig Pattern

Each student will need one copy of this page.

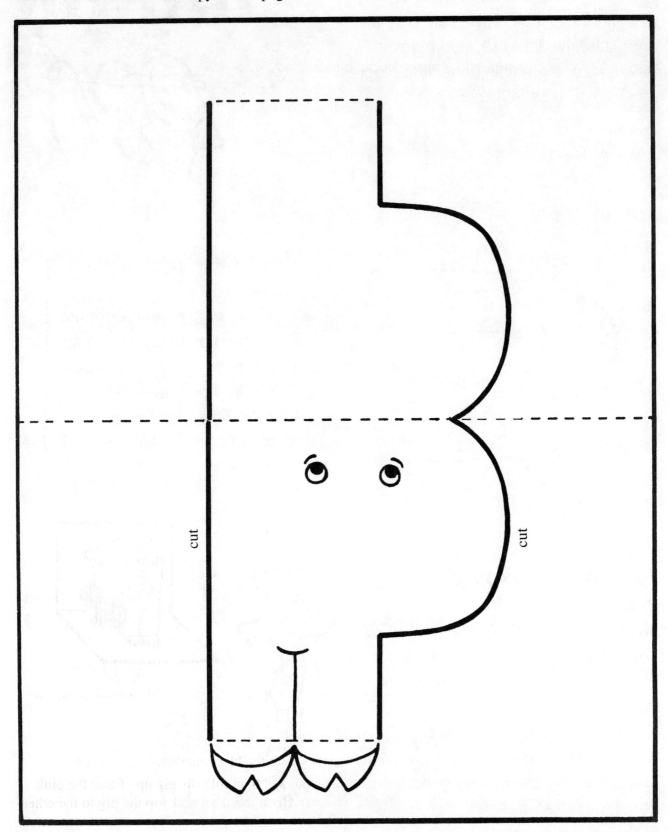

Song and Fingerplays for Pp

One Little, Two Little, Three Little Piggies

(Sing to the tune of "Ten Little Indians.")
One little, two little, three little piggies,
Four little, five little, six little piggies,
Seven little, eight little, nine little piggies,
Ten little piggies in a row.

This Little Piggy

(Traditional)
This little piggy went to market,
This little piggy stayed home.
This little piggy had roast beef,
This little piggy had none.
And this little piggy went
"Wee, wee, wee," all the way home.

Pop Goes the Weasel

(Traditional)
All around the cobbler's bench
The monkey chased the weasel,
The monkey thought 'twas all in fun,
Pop! Goes the weasel.
A penny for a spool of thread
A penny for a needle,
That's the way the money goes,
Pop! Goes the weasel.

Songs and Fingerplays for Pp *(cont.)*

Paw-Paw Patch

(Traditional)

(**Note:** *A paw paw is the largest edible fruit native to America.*
It grows on trees and can be up to 6" [15 cm] long.)

Where, oh where, is dear little Patty?
Where, oh where, is dear little Patty?
Where, oh where, is dear little Patty?
Way down yonder in the paw-paw patch.

Pickin' up paw-paws, put 'em in your pocket,
Pickin' up paw-paws, put 'em in your pocket
Pickin' up paw-paws, put 'em in your pocket
Way down yonder in the paw-paw patch.

Polly Wolly Doodle All the Day

(Traditional)

Oh, I went down South
For to see my Sal
Sing Polly wolly doodle all the day
My Sal, she is a spunky gal
Sing Polly wolly doodle all the day.
Fare thee well, fare thee well,
Fare thee well, my fairy fay
For I'm going to Lou'siana for to see
my Susyanna
Sing Polly wolly doodle all the day.

My Pocket Book for Pp

pig   1

pen   2

The pig is in the pen.   3

Qq

quack • queen • quilt

Story Books

Eight Hands Round, A Patchwork Alphabet
   by Ann Whitford Paul
Giggle, Giggle, Quack by Doreen Cronin and Betsy Lewin
The Keeping Quilt by Patricia Polacco
May I Bring a Friend? by Beatrice Schenk de Regniers
Q Is for Duck, An Alphabet Guessing Game
   by Mary Elfing
Quick as a Cricket by Don and Audrey Wood
Quick, Quack, Quick! by Marsha Diane Arnold
The Quilt by Ann Jonas
Selina and the Bear Paw Quilt by Barbara Smucker
The Very Quiet Cricket by Eric Carle

Foods/Snacks

- cheese slices, cut in quarters and put on crackers
- milk or juice from a quart container
- quarter of a cookie
- quarter of an apple
- quick (instant) pudding

Getting Started

1. Introduce the letter and the special picture. Read a book with the letter **Q** in the title. Brainstorm a list of other words that begin with a **Qq** and write the words on a chart. Include the names of any children in the class whose names begin with **Q**. (**Note:** When introducing the students to any of the activities or worksheets connected to the letter, the emphasis should be on the connection to the letter and the letter sound.)

2. Put a tissue-paper flame in one end of an empty toilet paper or paper towel tube. Put the paper tube on the floor to represent a candlestick. Recite the poem below and have students take turns jumping over the "candlestick."

Jack Be Nimble
Jack be nimble
Jack be quick
Jack jump over the candlestick.

Language Arts for Qq

Quotation Marks

Materials

- chart paper and marker
- elbow macaroni
- glue
- scissors
- construction paper
- crayons or markers

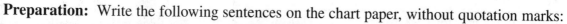

Preparation: Write the following sentences on the chart paper, without quotation marks:

- The ducks said, Quack, quack.
- I am quick, said the boy.
- This is a quiet game, said the girl.
- See my quilt, said the woman.
- I am the queen, said the queen.
- I have a quarter, said the man.

Procedure

1. Teach about quotation marks that are used to show that people are talking.
2. Cut the chart paper apart to make sentence strips. Glue the sentence strips on construction paper.
3. Glue the elbow macaroni where the quotation marks go.
4. Use crayons or markers to draw pictures to illustrate the sentences and display with the title, "Quotation Marks."

Describing Phrases

Materials

- *Quick As a Cricket* by Don and Audrey Wood
- chart paper and marker
- white sheets of construction paper (one per child)
- crayons or markers

Procedure

1. Use the following words to brainstorm a few phrases and write them on the chart paper.

   Funny as a _____.

   Tall as a _____.

   Loud as a _____.

   > Funny as a __clown__.
   > Funny as a __puppy__.
   > Funny as a __cartoon__.
   >
   > Tall as a __tree__.
   > Tall as a __giraffe__.
   > Tall as a __building__.
   >
   > Loud as a __jet__.
   > Loud as a __firecracker__.
   > Loud as a __rocket__.

2. Read the book, *Quick As a Cricket,* and discuss some of the phrases.
3. Add more phrases to the chart.
4. Draw pictures to illustrate the phrases.

Name _____

Printing Practice for Qq

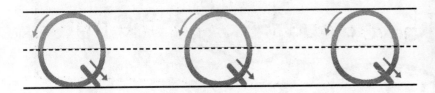

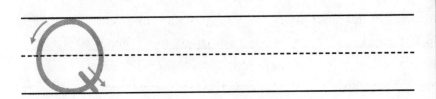

queen

Word Practice for Qq

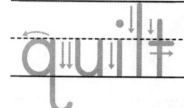

queen

quilt

quack

A duck can quack.

Science Activities for Qq

Quicksand

Hide objects in watery sand and read a book about quicksand.

Materials

- *The Quicksand Book* by Tomie dePaola
- sand
- water
- plastic dishpan
- small plastic toys
- chart paper and marker

Preparation: Draw a line down the center of the chart. Write the words "What we think we might find" at the top left, and the words, "What we found" at the top right. Put a layer of sand in the dishpan. Pour in enough water to just barely cover the sand. Press small plastic toys under the sand.

Procedure

1. Tell students that they are going to learn some information about quicksand. Explain that the dishpan has sand and water in it; it is not really quicksand.
2. Ask students to predict what they might find in the sand, and write predictions on the left side of the chart.
3. Read *The Quicksand Book* by Tomie dePaola.
4. Let students reach into the sand and withdraw one object at a time.
5. Write what they find on the right side of the chart.

Quicksand Looks Like a Solid, But Acts Like a Liquid!

Materials

- *Quicksand Question* by Ron Roy
- cornstarch
- water
- plastic bowl
- spoon

Procedure

1. Put the cornstarch in the bowl.
2. Add water and stir with a spoon until it makes a smooth paste. Advise students to pretend the mixture is quicksand.
3. Try rolling it into a ball. Discuss the results.
4. Put your hand flat on the surface. Discuss the results.
5. Poke fingers into the mixture. Discuss the results.
6. Read the book, *Quicksand Question*.

Art Activities for Qq

Qq Is for Quack

Materials

- duck pattern (page 175)
- sheets of white cardstock (one per child)
- white paper for speech bubbles
- yellow, white, brown, orange, and black paint
- paintbrushes
- scissors
- pencils

Preparation: Duplicate the duck and speech bubble patterns onto cardstock for each child.

Procedure

1. Use pencils to write or trace "quack, quack" in the speech bubble.
2. Paint the ducks in a variety of colors.
3. When the ducks are dry, use the scissors to cut out the ducks and speech bubbles.
4. Display with a title, Ducks say, "Quack, quack."

Quilts

Materials

- *The Quilt* by Ann Jonas, *The Josefina Story Quilt* by Eleanor Coerr, *The Keeping Quilt* by Patricia Polacco, *Eight Hands Round, A Patchwork Alphabet* by Valerie Flourney et al., and *The Quilt Story* by Tony Johnston
- 9" x 9" (23 cm x 23 cm) squares of light-colored fabric (one per child)
- quilts
- permanent markers
- thread
- scissors
- fabric for quilt backing
- binding to finish the edge
- sewing machine (optional)

Procedure

1. Show a quilt or two to the group and discuss how quilts are made of pieces of fabric sewn together.
2. Ask students to share quilts from home.
3. Read one or two of the books and discuss some of the names of the quilt patterns.
4. Draw on the squares of fabric with permanent markers.
5. Ask for parent or other volunteers to sew the squares together, put the backing on, and bind the quilt.

Qq Is for Quack

Duck Pattern

Each student will need one copy of this page.

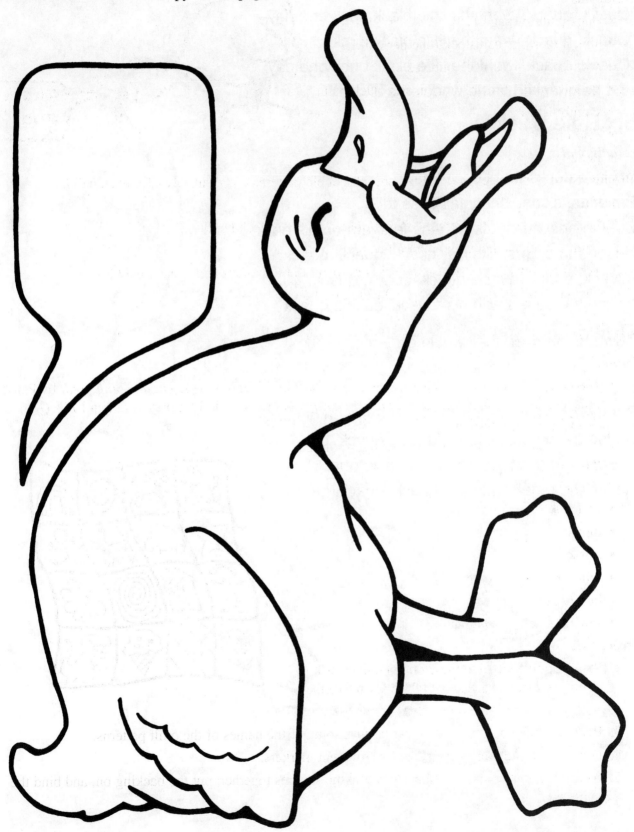

Songs and Fingerplays for Qq

"Quack, Quack," Went the Little Black Duck

(Traditional)

"Quack, quack," went the little black duck one day,

"Quack, quack," went the little black duck.

"Quack, quack," went the little black duck one day,

And he quacked as he waddled along.

Six Little Ducks

(Traditional)

Six little ducks that I once knew,

Fat ones, skinny ones, tall ones too.

But the one little duck with the feathers on his back,

He led the others with his "quack, quack, quack."

"Quack, quack, quack, quack, quack, quack."

He led the others with his "quack, quack, quack."

Down to the river, they would go,

Wibble, wobble, wibble, wobble,

to and fro.

But the one little duck with the feathers on his back,

He led the others with his "quack, quack, quack."

"Quack, quack, quack, quack, quack, quack."

He led the others with his "quack, quack, quack."

My Pocket Book for Qq

Qq

queen 1

quilt 2

The queen has a quilt. 3

Rr

rabbit • ride • run

Story Books

Little Red Riding Hood by Harriet Ziefert

My Friend Rabbit by Eric Rohmann

Rabbits, Rabbits and More Rabbits! by Gail Gibbons

A Rainbow of My Own by Don Freeman

Rooster's Off to See the World by Eric Carle

Rosie's Walk by Pat Hutchins

Rotten Ralph by Jack Gantos

Rumplestiltskin by Paul Galdone

Runaway Bunny by Margaret Wise Brown

The Tale of Peter Rabbit by Beatrix Potter

Foods/Snacks

- radishes
- raisins
- rice
- rice cereal treats
- rolls with raspberry jam
- rye bread

Getting Started

1. Introduce the letter and the special picture. Read a book with the letter **R** in the title. Brainstorm a list of other words that begin with an **Rr** and write the words on a chart. Include the names of any children in the class whose names begin with **R**. (**Note:** When introducing the students to any of the activities or worksheets connected to the letter, the emphasis should be on the connection to the letter and the letter sound.)

2. Play a game of Red Light, Green Light. One leader is chosen and stands in front of the group behind the finish line. The rest of the students line up at the opposite end of the play area. The leader turns around so that she or he cannot see the runners. The leader says, "Green light," and the runners run toward the leader. When the leader says, "Red light," all the runners must stop. Any runner who does not stop must go back to the start. When the leader says, "Green light" again, the runners go forward. The first student to run past the leader is the next leader. The rest of the students go back to the starting line.

3. Other activities for active play could be running, relay races, and hopping like rabbits.

Language Arts for Rr

Rhyming Words

Materials

- *One Fish, Two Fish, Red Fish, Blue Fish* or *Green Eggs and Ham* by Dr. Seuss
- rhyming word and picture cards (page 180–181)
- two sheets of white cardstock
- chart paper and marker
- nursery rhymes (two or three)

Preparation: Write nursery rhymes on charts (suggestions: "Little Boy Blue," "Jack and Jill," "Hey Diddle Diddle" and "Humpty Dumpty"). Duplicate a copy of the rhyming words and picture cards onto cardstock.

Procedure

1. Discuss that words rhyme because their endings have the same sound.
2. Read a book with many rhyming words.
3. Reread the book and stop to let students identify the rhyming words.
4. Go through the cards with rhyming pictures and identify all the pictures.
5. Put the cards in the chalk tray or on the floor and have students find the pairs of rhyming words or pictures.

Rock Collecting

Materials

- *Let's Go Rock Collecting* by Roma Gans
- egg cartons
- small rocks

Procedure

1. Read the book, *Let's Go Rock Collecting*.
2. Encourage students to collect small rocks and keep them in egg cartons.
3. Have students bring their rocks to school and compare rocks and trade with others. Talk about where certain rocks were found.
4. Display the rock collections with the title, "Rocks and More Rocks." Describe the colors and shapes. Lable as many rocks as possible.

Rhyming Words

Rhyming Word Cards

You will need one copy of this page for your class.

dish	spoon
fish	moon
cat	hair
hat	chair
jar	bee
car	tree

Rhyming Words *(cont.)*

Rhyming Picture Cards

You will need one copy of this page for your class.

hand	band	rock
sock	goat	boat
pen	men	star
jar	pan	man

Name _____

Printing Practice for Rr

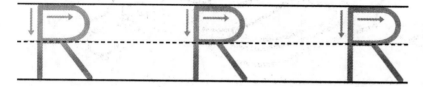

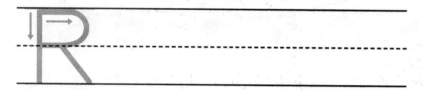

rabbit

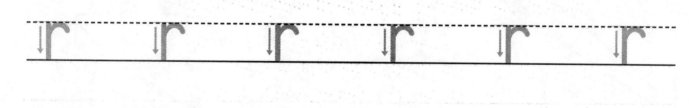

Name _____

Word Practice for Rr

rabbit

ride

run

Rabbits can run.

Science Activities for Rr

Raisin Experiment

Materials

- ginger ale or clear soda
- clear, tall plastic cups (one per student)
- raisins
- chart paper and marker
- drawing paper (one page per student)
- pencils

Procedure

1. Show students a glass of ginger ale and a handful of raisins.
2. Ask students what will happen when you put the raisins in the ginger ale. Write the title "What We Think Will Happen" on the chart, and students' responses below the title.
3. Distribute plastic cups, ginger ale, and raisins to each student.
4. Watch the raisins. As bubbles collect on the raisins, some will rise to the top, the bubbles will pop, and the raisins will sink to the bottom. Others will rise to the top. (Why? Because the air in the bubbles weighs less than the soda.)
5. Use paper and pencils to draw a picture of what is happening with the raisins.
6. On the chart, write "What Happened," and record students' observations.
7. Display pictures and the chart with the title, "Dancing Raisins."

Rainbows with Prisms

Materials

- *A Rainbow of My Own* by Don Freeman
- prisms
- sunny window
- crayons
- sheets of drawing paper (one per child)

Procedure

1. Read the book and discuss how the rainbow was made.
2. Use a prism to make a rainbow. Show how you have to look around to find the rainbow.
3. Have students experiment with the prisms.
4. Draw pictures of the prisms and the rainbows.
5. Put a prism in the science center for independent exploration.

Art Activities for Rr

Rabbits

Materials

- rabbit and carrot patterns (page 186)
- discarded wallpaper books
- pencils
- double-sided tape
- scissors
- orange and green markers or crayons
- cotton balls
- sheets of construction paper (one per child)
- glue

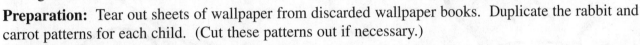

Preparation: Tear out sheets of wallpaper from discarded wallpaper books. Duplicate the rabbit and carrot patterns for each child. (Cut these patterns out if necessary.)

Procedure

1. Use scissors to cut out the parts of the rabbit and the carrot.
2. Put a little bit of double-sided tape on the backside of the rabbit pattern pieces and place them on a sheet of wallpaper.
3. Cut around the patterns and discard the pattern and the tape.
4. Let the students decide where to place the rabbit parts on the construction paper.
5. Glue the cotton ball over the tail.
6. Color the carrot with the orange and green markers and glue on the paper.
7. Display the pictures with the title, "Rabbits, Rabbits, Rabbits."

Rainbow Paintings

Materials

- *Planting a Rainbow* by Lois Ehlert
- colored plastic toys in the colors of a rainbow
- chart paper and colored markers
- pencil
- scissors
- glue
- red, orange, yellow, green, blue, indigo, and violet paint
- paintbrushes
- sheets of white construction paper (one per child)

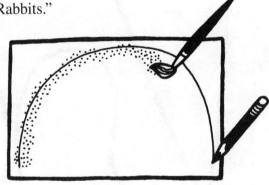

Preparation: Draw an arch on each sheet of construction paper using a pencil (in shape of rainbow).

Procedure

1. Show the students the toys and have them identify the colors.
2. Write each color word on the chart using the appropriate color.
3. Read the book, *Planting a Rainbow*.
4. Cut the color words apart and paste them in the order of a rainbow on a new chart.
5. Paint the pencil line in red and let dry. Continue painting each color under the previous one using the chart as a guide.
6. Display the painting.

Rabbits

Rabbit and Carrot Patterns

Each student will need one copy of this page.

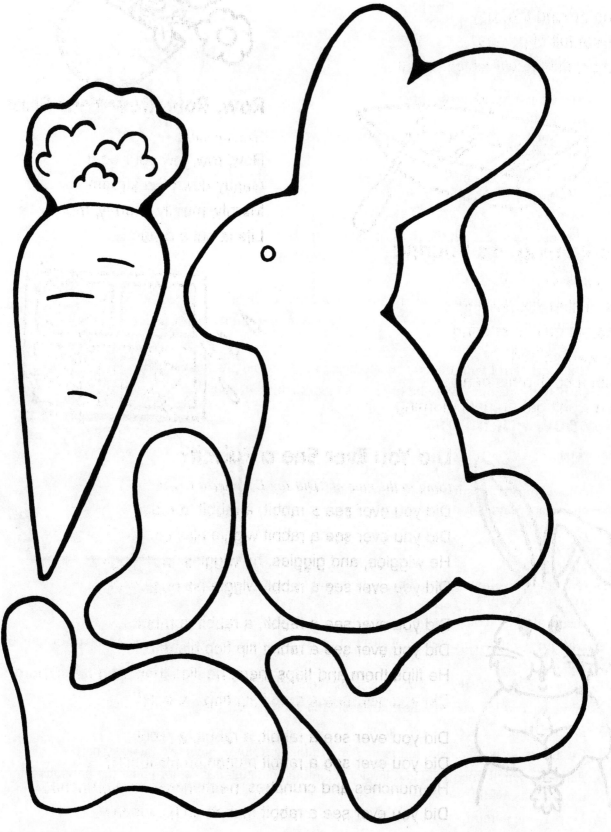

Songs and Fingerplays for Rr

Ring Around the Rosy

(Traditional)

Ring around the rosy
Pocket full of posies,
Ashes, ashes, we all fall down!

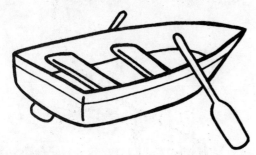

Row, Row, Row Your Boat

(Traditional)

Row, row, row your boat
Gently down the stream
Merrily, merrily, merrily, merrily
Life is but a dream!

It's Raining, It's Pouring

(Traditional)

It's raining, it's pouring
The old man is snoring
He went to bed
With a cold in his head
And won't get up until morning.

Did You Ever See a Rabbit?

(Sing to the tune of "Did You Ever See a Lassie?")

Did you ever see a rabbit, a rabbit, a rabbit,
Did you ever see a rabbit wiggle his nose?
He wiggles, and giggles, he wiggles, and giggles.
Did you ever see a rabbit wiggle his nose?

Did you ever see a rabbit, a rabbit, a rabbit,
Did you ever see a rabbit flip flop his ears?
He flips them and flaps them, he flips them and flaps them,
Did you ever see a rabbit flip flop his ears?

Did you ever see a rabbit, a rabbit, a rabbit
Did you ever see a rabbit munch on his lunch?
He munches and crunches, he munches and crunches,
Did you ever see a rabbit munch on his lunch?

Songs and Fingerplays for Rr (cont.)

Little Robin Redbreast Sat Upon a Tree

(Traditional)

Little Robin Redbreast sat upon a tree,

Up went pussy cat, and down went he!

Down came pussy, and away Robin ran;

Says little Robin Redbreast, "Catch me if you can!"

Little Robin Redbreast jumped upon a wall,

Pussy cat jumped after him, and almost got a fall!

Little Robin chirped and sang, and what did pussy say?

Pussy cat said, "Meow," and Robin jumped away.

I've Been Working on the Railroad

(Traditional)

I've been working on the railroad,

All the live long day

I've been working on the railroad

Just to pass the time away.

Can't you hear the whistle blowing,

Rise up so early in the morn'

Can't you hear the captain shouting

Dinah, blow your horn.

Dinah, won't you blow

Dinah, won't you blow,

Dinah, won't you blow your h-or-orn

Dinah, won't you blow

Dinah, won't you blow,

Dinah, won't you blow your horn?

Someone's in the kitchen with Dinah,

Someone's in the kitchen I know-o-o-o

Someone's in the kitchen with Dinah,

Strummin' on the old banjo.

And singing fee-fi-fiddley-i-o

Fee-fi-fiddley-i-o-o-o-o

Fee-fi-fiddley-i-o

Strummin' on the old banjo.

My Pocket Book for Rr

R r

rabbit 1

run 2

See the rabbit run. 3

Ss

star • stop • sun

Story Books

Our Stars by Anne Rockwell

The Reasons for Seasons by Gail Gibbons

Sammy the Seal by Syd Hoff

Slowly, Slowly, Said the Sloth by Eric Carle

Snakes Are Hunters by Patricia Lauber

Song and Dance Man by Karen Ackerman

Stone Soup by Marcia Brown

Strega Nona by Tomie dePaola

Swimmy by Leo Lionni

The Very Busy Spider by Eric Carle

Foods/Snacks

- sandwiches
- spaghetti
- "stone" soup
- strawberries
- strawberry gelatin
- sunflower seeds

Getting Started

1. Introduce the letter and the special picture. Read a book with the letter **S** in the title. Brainstorm a list of other words that begin with an **Ss** and write the words on a chart. Include the names of any children in the class whose names begin with **S**. (**Note:** When introducing the students to any of the activities or worksheets connected to the letter, the emphasis should be on the connection to the letter and the letter sound.)

2. Play a game of Simon Says. The students stand up where they will have plenty of wiggle room. Model being a leader. When the leader says, "Simon says," the correct response is to follow the direction. But if the direction is given without saying "Simon says," the direction is ignored. If a student follows that type of direction, then he or she has to sit down. Depending on the age of the students, the last person to be left standing is the new leader. If the child is too young to be the leader, the teacher can continue to lead the game.

   Directions might include the following:

   - Simon says, "Put your hands on your head." Simon says, "Put your fingers on your toes."

   - "Put your hands on your hips." (If a student responds to this direction, he or she must sit down and wait for a new game to begin.)

Language Arts for Ss

I See Something . . .

Materials

- eight sentence strips
- sheets of white construction paper (one per child)
- crayons or markers
- stapler

Preparation: Prepare the sentence strips with the words as follows: I see something *red*. I see something *orange*. I see something *yellow*. I see something *green*. I see something *blue*. I see something *purple*. I see something *brown*. I see something *black*. (**Note:** The color words should be printed in the correct color for easy identification.) On each sheet of paper, write the sentence starter.

I see something _____ .

Procedure

1. Teach the students to read the sentence strips and practice reading them.

2. Put the sentence strips around the room and choose a student to start the game.

3. The student will choose an object, find the sentence strip with the correct color, and hold up the sentence strip so the other students can read it. He or she will then call on a student to guess the chosen object.

4. If a student identifies the object correctly, he or she is the new leader.

5. After three guesses, if no one has guessed what the object is, the leader will identify the object and choose a new leader.

6. Give each student a sheet with the sentence starter.

7. Write the color word the student chooses on the sheet and have the student draw a picture with that one color. Label the pictures with the name of the object.

8. Put the sheets together, add the cover with a title, and staple the pages together.

9. Share the book by having each student stand and read his or her page.

10. Put the book in the reading center.

Name _____

Printing Practice for Ss

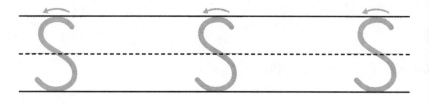

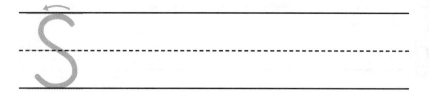

sun

Name _____

Word Practice for Ss

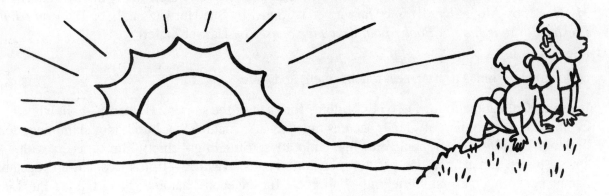

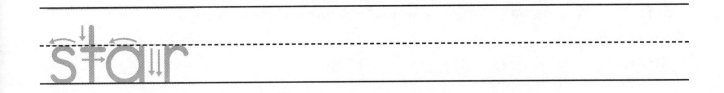

sun

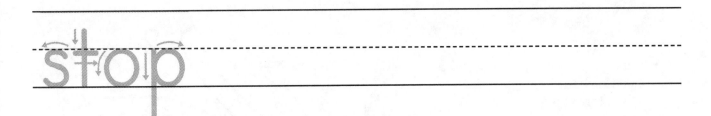

star

stop

We see the sun.

Science Activities for Ss

Five Senses

Materials

- *My Five Senses* by Aliki, *The Five Senses* by Keith Faulkner, *The Listening Walk* by Paul Showers, *My Hands* by Aliki, *Sight* by Sue Hurwitz et al., *Smell* by Sue Hurwitz et al., or *You Can't Tell a Pickle with Your Ear: A Book About Your Five Senses* by Harriet Ziefert

- boxes with lids

- collections of things to hear, see, touch, smell, and taste

Preparation: Collect the following types of items for each of the senses. **Hearing**—bell, whistle, cymbals, tape recording of sounds such as music, water running, car horn, door slamming, dog barking. **Seeing**—poster, book, drawing, lamp, toys. **Smelling**—empty film canisters with spices, herbs, and extracts and perfumes on cotton balls. **Tasting**—fruit slices, cut-up vegetables, candy, popcorn, crackers. **Touching**—ball, rock, fur, pinecone, hammer, silky fabric. Put the objects in a "feely box" with the lid taped shut and a hole large enough for a student to put in a hand to feel the objects.

Procedure

1. Explain that we use our five senses to learn more about things. Name the five senses—hearing, seeing, touching, tasting, and smelling.
2. Read a book about the five senses.
3. One at a time, share the collections listed above to show the importance of the five senses.
4. Use the "feely box" to show the importance of touching.
5. Put the collections and the box in the science center for students to examine.

Stone Soup

Materials

- *Stone Soup* by Marcia Brown
- note to parents
- large kettle
- stove or slow cooker
- beef bouillon
- vegetables
- water
- clean rock
- spoon for stirring
- plastic cups, spoons, napkins (one per child)
- chart paper and marker

Preparation: Write and duplicate a note to parents to request one washed, peeled, and diced vegetable sent to school on the day of the activity.

Procedure

1. Read the book and put the rock in the pot.
2. Put the vegetables in the pot with water and the bouillon.
3. Make a list of all the ingredients and circle each **s**.
4. Cook until the vegetables are soft.
5. Cool slightly, serve in cups, and enjoy.

Art Activities for Ss

Sun Paintings

Materials

- *Rooster's Off to See the World, The Very Hungry Caterpillar, The Tiny Seed, Does a Kangaroo Have a Mother, Too?* and *The Mixed Up Chameleon* by Eric Carle
- yellow, red, and orange paint
- shallow dishes for paint
- paintbrushes
- easel paper and easels (if possible)
- newspaper

Procedure

1. Read several of the books by Eric Carle and point out the suns he puts in his books. Describe the suns. What shapes are used? What kinds of lines and colors are used?
2. Distribute large sheets of paper.
3. Model how to start the paintings by painting a large yellow circle and rays going out from the circle.
4. While the yellow is still wet, use a little red and orange paint and mix the colors right on the paper.
5. Paint a smiling face on the sun.
6. Rinse out the paintbrushes for the next person.
7. When the paintings are dry, display with the title, "See Our Suns."

String Art

Materials

- eight aluminum pie pans
- red, orange, yellow, green, blue, purple, brown, and black paint
- string
- paper
- newspaper

Preparation: Cut the string into lengths long enough to go across and hang over the edges of the pie pans. Put enough paint in the pie pans to cover the bottom of the pans. Put a string over each pan of paint.

Procedure

1. Dip the string into the paint. Pick it up and lay down the string on the paper while still holding onto both ends.
2. Repeat the dipping process several times with each color.
3. When dry, display the string art pictures with the title, "See Our String Pictures."

Art Activities for Ss *(cont.)*

Seed Pictures

Materials

- *The Carrot Seed* by Crockett Johnson, *The Tiny Seed* by Eric Carle, *How a Seed Grows* by Helene J. Jordan, and *From Seed to Plant* by Gail Gibbons
- variety of dried seeds (kidney beans, split peas, lentils, lima beans, navy beans, black beans)
- magnifying glasses
- shallow plastic cups
- glue in a squeeze bottle with a narrow tip
- heavy paper or cardboard
- knife to split seeds

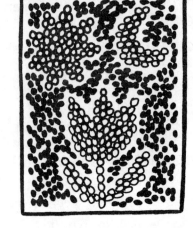

Procedure

1. Read books about seeds.
2. Split a few dried seeds and find the little plant inside.
3. Look at the little plant with magnifying glasses.
4. Distribute paper, glue, and a variety of seeds in the plastic cups.
5. Create a seed mosaic on the heavy paper.

Star Drawings

Materials

- *Draw Me a Star* by Eric Carle
- chart paper and marker
- pencils
- paper

Procedure

1. Read the book, *Draw Me a Star.*
2. Demonstrate how to draw a star on the chart paper.
3. Have students draw a star on the paper while it is being demonstrated.

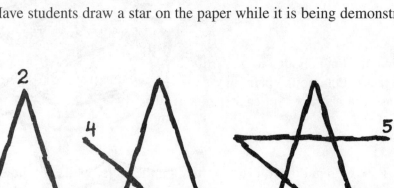

Songs and Fingerplays for Ss

See Saw Marjorie Daw

(Traditional)

See Saw Marjorie Daw
Suzie shall have a new master
She shall work for a penny a day
Because she can't work any faster.

See Saw Marjorie Daw
Sammy shall have a new master
He shall work for a penny a day
Because he can't work any faster.

Sailing, Sailing

(Traditional)

Sailing, sailing
O'er the bounding main
For many a stormy wind shall blow
E'er Jack comes home again.

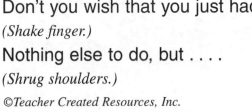

Swimming, Swimming

(Sing to the tune of "Sailing, Sailing.")

Swimming, swimming
(Paddle arms.)
In a swimming pool
(Make rectangle with hands.)
The weather's hot, the water's cold
(Wipe brow and shiver.)
In my swimming pool.
(Make rectangle with hands.)
Side stroke, breast stroke,
(Stroke to side, then front.)
Fancy diving, too.
(Put hands together and dive.)
Don't you wish that you just had
(Shake finger.)
Nothing else to do, but . . . .
(Shrug shoulders.)

Songs and Fingerplays for Ss *(cont.)*

Sippity Sup

(Traditional)

Sippity sup, sippity sup
Bread and milk from a china cup
Bread and milk on a bright silver spoon
Made of a piece of the bright silver moon
Sippity sup, sippity sup
Sippity sippity sup.

Star Light, Star Bright

(Traditional)

Star light, star bright
First star I've seen tonight,
Wish I may, wish I might
Have the wish I wish tonight.

Simple Simon

(Traditional)

Simple Simon met a pieman,
Going to the fair.

Said Simple Simon to the pieman.
"Let me taste your ware."

Said the pieman unto Simon,
"Show me first your penny."

Said Simple Simon to the pieman,
"Indeed I have not any."

My Pocket Book for Ss

S s

sun

1

star

2

The sun is a star.

3

Tt

teeth • tree • turtle

Story Books

Arthur's Tooth by Marc Brown

Be a Friend to Trees by Patricia Lauber

Franklin Plants a Tree by Paulette Bourgeois

Freight Train by Donald Crews

Little Toot by Hardie Gramatky

Sam and the Tigers by Julius Lester

Sea Turtles by Gail Gibbons

Teddy Bear, Teddy Bear by Michael Hague

Teeny Tiny Woman by Jane O'Connor

Tell Me, Tree by Gail Gibbons

Today Is Monday by Eric Carle

Foods/Snacks

- tangerines
- tea
- toast
- tuna fish
- turkey roll-ups

Getting Started

1. Introduce the letter and the special picture. Read a book with the letter **T** in the title. Brainstorm a list of other words that begin with a **Tt** and write the words on a chart. Include the names of any children in the class whose names begin with **T**. (**Note:** When introducing the students to any of the activities or worksheets connected to the letter, the emphasis should be on the connection to the letter and the letter sound.)

2. Go outside or to the gym and play a game of Tiptoe Tag. Play this game the same as Tag, but while staying on your tiptoes.

3. Read one of the suggested books about trees, or *Franklin Plants a Tree* by Paulette Bourgeois, and then go on a tree walk. Go outdoors to a place where there are several kinds of trees. Feel the bark of different kinds of trees. Remind the students that we do not take the bark off trees, but we can feel how rough it is. Take paper and brown crayons to sketch pictures of the trees or make crayon rubbings of the bark.

Language Arts for Tt

Take-off Book

Materials

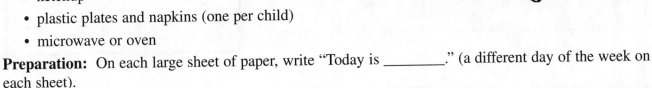

- *Today Is Monday* by Eric Carle
- chart paper and marker
- seven large sheets of heavy paper
- crayons or markers
- old magazines
- scissors
- glue
- stapler, comb binding, or binder rings
- Tater Tots®
- ketchup
- plastic plates and napkins (one per child)
- microwave or oven

Preparation: On each large sheet of paper, write "Today is _____." (a different day of the week on each sheet).

Procedure

1. Read *Today Is Monday* several times and sing the song listed in the back of the book.
2. Discuss the students' favorite foods and list them on chart paper.
3. Each student will find pictures of foods they like and cut them out.
4. Glue several pictures on each page with the words, "Today is _____."
5. Decorate the pages with crayons or markers.
6. Assemble the book so that the days of the week are in order.
7. Read the book aloud and let each student tell what the food is that he or she pasted on a page.
8. Reread the book several times and put it in the reading center.
9. Heat the Tater Tots® and put a few on each plate.
10. Have a Tater Tot Tasting with ketchup.

Printing Practice for Tt

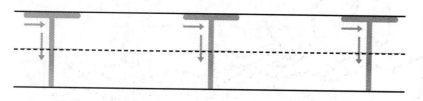

turtle

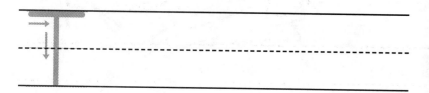

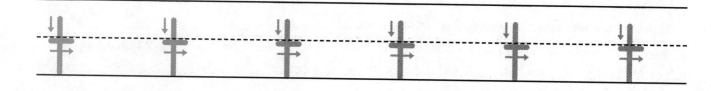

202

Name _____

Word Practice for Tt

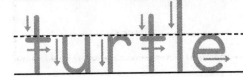
turtle

teeth

tree

I see a big turtle.

Science Activities for Tt

Teeth

Find out facts about teeth.

Materials

- *My Tooth Is Loose* by Martin Silverman, *Bear's Toothache* by David Mc Phail, or *The Tooth Book* by Theo LeSieg
- mirrors
- chart paper and marker
- dentist

Preparation: On the chart paper, write the title "We Take Care of Our Teeth."

Procedure

1. Read a book about teeth. Encourage students to use mirrors to observe their teeth.
2. Ask students if they have teeth that are loose or that have come out.
3. Ask students what they do to take care of their teeth. Write their responses on the chart.
4. Invite a dentist to come to discuss how important it is to take care of teeth.
5. Learn the song, "Brush, Brush, Brush Your Teeth" (page 208).

Trees

Discover how trees get water from the ground.

Materials

- *A Tree Is a Plant* by Clyde Robert Bulla, *Tell Me, Tree* by Gail Gibbons, or *Be a Friend to Trees* by Patricia Lauber
- pictures of trees
- 3 celery stalks
- 4 water glasses
- red and blue food coloring

Preparation: Dilute the food coloring with water.

Procedure

1. If possible, go outside for a walk and observe trees. Discuss different kinds, sizes, and shapes of trees. Look at pictures of trees.
2. Read a nonfiction book about trees.
3. Discuss how important water is to trees. Ask the question, "How does water get from the ground up into the leaves?"
4. Cut the bottoms off three stalks of celery. Leave the leaves on the stalks.
5. Add 1–2" (3–5 cm) of water and food coloring to each glass.
6. Place one celery stalk in a glass filled with water and blue food coloring and another celery stalk in a glass filled with water and red food coloring.
7. Split the third celery stalk down the middle. Do not cut it in half completely. Leave the leafy end intact. Place one side of the stalk in the second glass of red water and the other side of the stalk in the blue water.
8. Observe as the color rises in the stalks. Compare the experiment to trees outside.

Art Activities for Tt

Trains

Materials

- *Freight Train* by Donald Crews
- shoeboxes (one per child)
- note to parents
- sheets of construction paper or paint
  (red, orange, yellow, green, blue, purple, brown, and black)
- 2" (5 cm) wide black tagboard circles
- crayons or markers
- glue
- brads (optional)

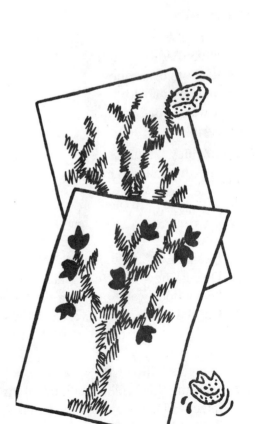

Preparation: Send a note home to parents to request shoeboxes.

Procedure

1. Read the book, *Freight Train*, and note the different kinds and colors of cars on the train.
3. Cover shoeboxes with many colors of construction paper or paint.
4. Attach the black circles on the shoeboxes for wheels.
5. Look at the book again and add details to the engine and cars using crayons or markers.

Tree Paintings

Materials

- large sheets of white construction paper (one per child)
- brown, black, and two or three shades of green paint
- flat plates or pans
- scissors
- sponges (regular and leaf patterns)
- paintbrushes
- newspaper

Preparation: Pour a small amount of paint onto the plates. Put the construction paper on plenty of newspaper.

Procedure

1. To make the trunk of the trees, sponge brown paint onto the paper. Then make branches using paintbrushes and the brown paint.
2. When the trunks and branches are dry, use the leaf sponges in several colors of green paint.
3. If this lesson is taught in the fall, the leaves could be painted in fall colors. If it is winter, the branches could be left bare.

Art Activities for Tt *(cont.)*

Turtles

Materials

- *Little Turtle and the Song of the Sea* by Sheridan Cain or *Sea Turtles* by Gail Gibbons
- 6" (15 cm) paper bowls
- green and black paint
- chart paper and markers
- paintbrushes
- turtle pattern (one per child)
- scissors
- stapler
- markers
- round sticker spots

Procedure

1. Read a book about turtles. After reading the book, ask students what they know about turtles.
2. Write turtle facts on chart paper.
3. Cut the chart about turtles apart to create sentence strips.
4. Display the turtles, the strips, and the title "See Our Turtles" on the bulletin board.

Turtle Assembly

1. Paint the bottom of the bowls green. Let them dry and then add details with black paint.

2. Cut out the turtle pattern and color it with markers.

3. Staple the pattern (at the legs) to the edges of the bowl.

4. Add the sticker spots and a face.

Songs and Fingerplays for Tt

There Was a Little Turtle

(Traditional)

There was a little turtle
Who lived in a box
He swam in the puddles
And climbed on the rocks.
He snapped at a mosquito
He snapped at a flea
He snapped at a minnow
And he snapped at me.
He caught the mosquito
He caught the flea
He caught the minnow
But he didn't catch me!

I'm a Little Teapot

(Traditional)

I'm a little teapot,
Short and stout.
Here is my handle,
Here is my spout.
When I get all steamed up,
Hear me shout,
Just tip me over and pour me out.

I'm a very clever pot
That's true
Here's an example
Of what I can do.
I can change my handle
And my spout.
Just tip me over and pour me out!

Songs and Fingerplays for Tt *(cont.)*

Twinkle, Twinkle Little Star

(Traditional)

Twinkle, twinkle little star
How I wonder where you are.
Up above the world so high
Like a diamond in the sky,
Twinkle, twinkle little star
How I wonder where you are.

Ride the Train

(Sing to the tune of "Row, Row, Row Your Boat.")

Ride, ride, ride the train
Ride it down the tracks
We will have such fun today
Now we're going back.

Brush, Brush, Brush Your Teeth

(Sing to the tune of "Row, Row, Row Your Boat.")

Brush, brush, brush your teeth,
Brush them every day
Brush and brush and brush and brush
That's the healthy way!

Floss, floss, floss your teeth,
Floss them every day
Floss and floss and floss and floss
That's the healthy way!

Rinse, rinse, rinse your teeth,
Rinse them every day
Rinse and rinse and rinse and rinse
That's the healthy way!

My Pocket Book for Tt

T t

turtle 1

tree 2

The turtle is by the tree. 3

Uu

umbrella • under • up

Story Books

Aunt Harriet's Underground Railroad in the Sky by Faith Ringgold

Great Day for Up! by Dr. Seuss

Inside, Outside, Upside Down by Stan Berenstain

Listen to the Rain by Bill Martin, Jr.

There's An Alligator Under My Bed by Mercer Mayer

The Ugly Duckling by Hans Christian Andersen

Umbrella by Taro Yashima

Umbrella Party by Janet Louise Lunn

Up and Down on the Merry-Go-Round by Bill Martin, Jr.

Yellow Umbrella by Jae-Soo Liu

Foods/Snacks

- ugli fruit (citrus from Jamaica)
- Uncle Sam's hat cake, with stars and stripes
- uncooked vegetables
- upside-down cake

Getting Started

1. Introduce the letter and the special picture. Read a book with the letter **U** in the title. Brainstorm a list of other words that begin with a **Uu** and write the words on a chart. Include the names of any children in the class whose names begin with **U**. (**Note:** When introducing the students to any of the activities or worksheets connected to the letter, the emphasis should be on the connection to the letter and the letter sound.)

2. Get up and move. Hold arms up in a **U** shape. Play music that encourages students to move in time to the music. Allow plenty of space for action.

3. Read the book, *Up and Down on the Merry-Go-Round* by Bill Martin, Jr. Arrange the students in a circle. Play music that sounds like a merry-go-round. Walk around in a circle and try to go up when the student in front of you is going down, and down when the student in front is going up.

Language Arts for Uu

Up or Under?

Materials
- worksheets (see below)   • pencils   • crayons

Preparation: Duplicate a copy of the worksheet below for each child.

Procedure
1. Teach the words, *up* and *under*.
2. Circle the correct word below each picture.
3. Color the pictures.

Name _____

Printing Practice for Uu

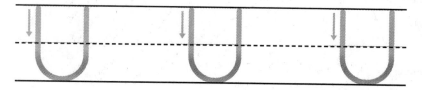

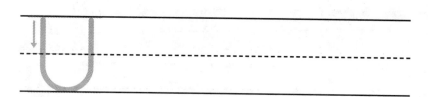

umbrella

Word Practice for Uu

umbrella

up

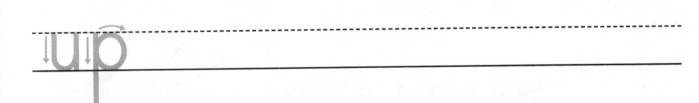

under

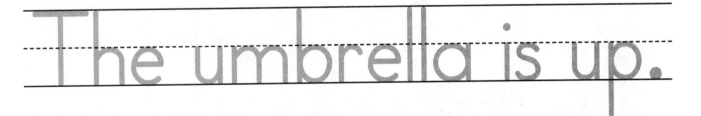

The umbrella is up.

Science Activity for Uu

Underground Animals

Materials

- *Wiggling Worms at Work* by Wendy Pfeffer
- underground (burrowing) animal patterns (see below)
- crayons and markers
- scissors
- long sheet of brown wrapping paper
- dried coffee grounds
- glue

Preparation: Enlarge and duplicate the underground (burrowing) animal patterns below for each child.

Procedure

1. Read a book about animals that live underground. Discuss how some animals live underground all or part of the time.
2. Color the animals and cut them out.
3. Glue the animals on the brown paper and draw the burrows and tunnels they would inhabit.
4. Spread glue on the paper and sprinkle with coffee grounds.
5. Display with the title, "Underground Animals."

Underground Animal Patterns

Art Activities for Uu

Umbrellas

Materials

- *Umbrella* by Taro Yashima
- umbrella
- umbrella pattern (page 216)
- sheets of white construction paper (one per child)
- crayons or markers
- scissors
- chenille sticks (one per child)
- glue or tape

Preparation: Duplicate the umbrella pattern onto construction paper for each child.

Procedure

1. Show an umbrella and discuss why we use umbrellas.
2. Read a book about umbrellas, and discuss umbrella usage and safety.
3. Decorate the umbrella pattern and cut it out.
4. Add the chenille stick for the handle. Use glue or tape to attach it.
5. When the pictures in the activity below are completed, glue the umbrellas on the mural.

Portraits of Us

Materials

- sheets of white construction paper (one per child)
- crayons or markers
- scissors
- glue
- light blue paint
- shallow pan
- brush with stiff bristles
- mural paper

Preparation: Pour the blue paint into a shallow pan.

Procedure

1. Each student draws and colors a picture of himself or herself with one arm up.
2. Cut out the figures.
3. Lay the mural paper flat. Dip the brush in the paint and splash (spatter) paint over the mural to look like rain.
4. Glue the pictures on the mural.
5. Let the mural dry and hang it up with the title, "Us Under Umbrellas."
6. Have each child add a decorated umbrella to his or her portrait on the mural.

Umbrella Mural

Umbrella Pattern

Each student will need one copy of this page duplicated on construction paper.

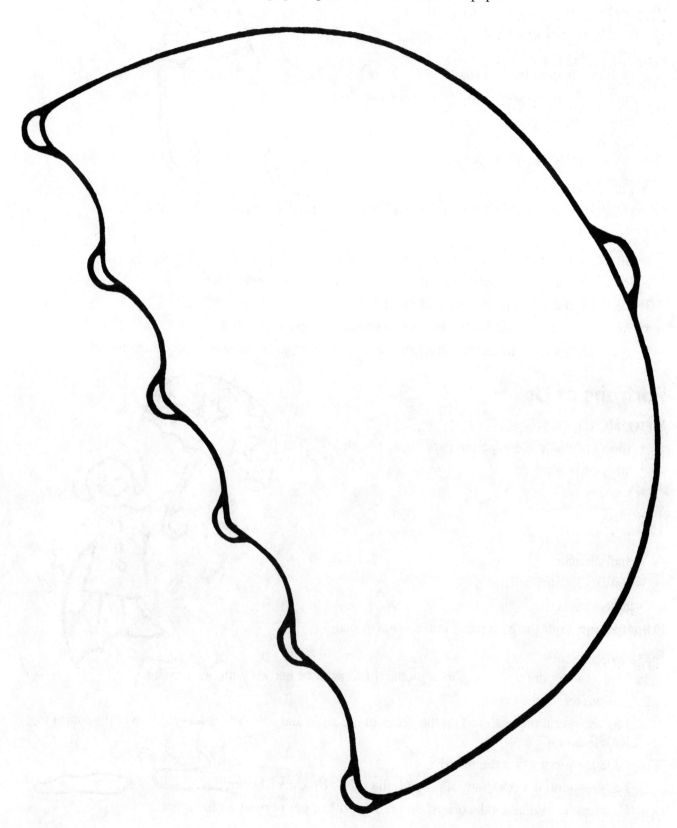

Songs and Fingerplays for Uu

The Grand Old Duke of York

The grand old Duke of York
He had ten thousand men
He marched them up a very high hill
(Stand up.)
And he marched them down again.
(Squat down.)
But when you're up, you're up
(Stand up.)
And when you're down you're down
(Squat down.)
But when you're only half-way up
(Start to stand up.)
You're neither up nor down!
(Stand up, then sit down.)

The Rain on the Umbrellas

(Sing to the tune of "The Wheels on the Bus.")
The rain on the umbrellas
    goes drip, drip, drip,
Drip, drip, drip,
    drip, drip, drip,
The rain on the umbrellas
    goes drip, drip, drip,
All through the town.

The sun on the umbrellas
    goes shine, shine, shine,
Shine, shine, shine,
    shine, shine, shine,
The sun on the umbrellas
    goes shine, shine, shine,
All through the town.

My Pocket Book for Uu

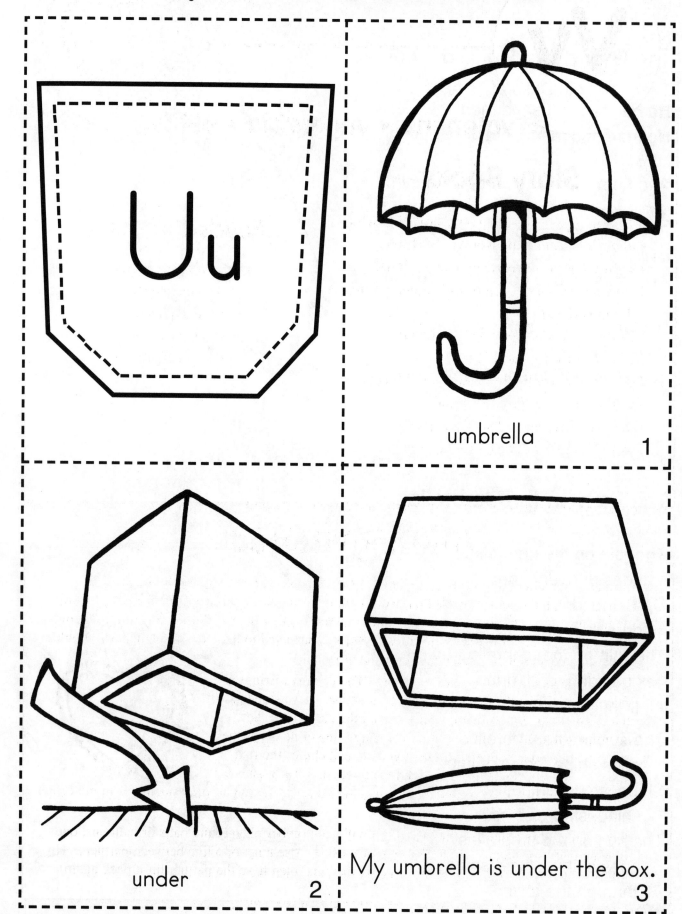

umbrella

1

under

2

My umbrella is under the box.

3

Vv

valentine • vegetable • vet

Story Books

A Charlie Brown Valentine by Charles M. Schulz

Clifford's Valentines by Norman Bridwell

The Day It Rained Hearts by Felicia Bond

Eating the Alphabet: Fruits and Vegetables from A to Z by Lois Ehlert

Growing Vegetable Soup by Lois Ehlert

Hill of Fire by Thomas P. Lewis

Little Bear's Visit by Else Homelund Minarik

The Valentine Bears by Eve Bunting

Valentine Mice! by Bethany Roberts

The Very Lonely Firefly by Eric Carle

Foods/Snacks

- valentine hearts
- vanilla cookies
- vanilla pudding
- vegetable soup
- veggies and dip

Getting Started

1. Introduce the letter and the special picture. Read a book with the letter **V** in the title. Brainstorm a list of other words that begin with a **Vv** and write the words on a chart. Include the names of any children in the class whose names begin with **V**. (**Note:** When introducing the students to any of the activities or worksheets connected to the letter, the emphasis should be on the connection to the letter and the letter sound.)

2. Teach students the first verse of the song, "The Postman Brings a Valentine" (page 226). You will need a valentine. Have students sit in a large circle. One student walks around the circle with the valentine while all the students sing the song. She or he drops the valentine behind a student, who then gets up and chases the first student. The first student runs around the circle until he or she can sit in the spot where the second student had been sitting. If caught, the student sits in the center until someone else is caught.

3. Play a game of beginning volleyball. You will need rubber playground balls or balloons, one for each pair of students. Go to the gym or outside. Use a net or a line between partners. Hit or throw the ball over the net or line to a partner, and then have the partner hit it back again.

Language Arts for Vv

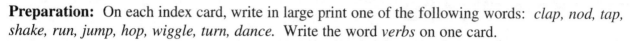

Verbs

Materials

- 11 large index cards
- chart paper and marker
- tape

Preparation: On each index card, write in large print one of the following words: *clap, nod, tap, shake, run, jump, hop, wiggle, turn, dance.* Write the word *verbs* on one card.

Procedure

1. Sing the following song.
   "If You're Happy and You Know It, Clap Your Hands."

   If you're happy and you know it, clap your hands,

   If you're happy and you know it, clap your hands,

   If you're happy and you know it, then your face will surely show it,

   If you're happy and you know it, clap your hands.

(**Note:** Verse 2—nod your head, Verse 3—tap your toe, Verse 4—do all three.)

2. Share a few of the cards and explain that other actions can take the place of the ones in the song.
3. Hold up one card at a time and have students perform the appropriate action.
4. Tape the cards to the wall or chalkboard.
5. Explain that action words are called "verbs."
6. When all of the cards have been shown, the actions performed, and the cards taped to the wall, let a student take a card from the wall and hold it up. Read the action and sing the song. Repeat several times.
7. Tape the verb cards to the chart paper.
8. Ask students to suggest other verbs and write them on the chart.
9. Suggest that verbs be used when writing.

Name _____

Printing Practice for Vv

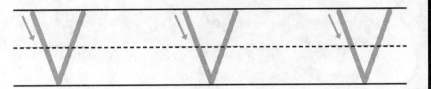

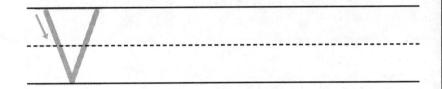

valentine

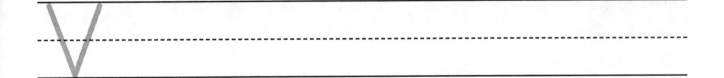

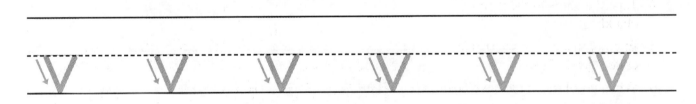

Name _____

Word Practice for Vv

valentine

vegetable

vet

I eat vegetables.

Science Activity for Vv

Volcanoes

Materials

- *Volcanoes* by Franklyn Branley, *Volcanoes: Mountains That Blew Their Tops* by Nicholas Nirgiotis, or *Hill of Fire* by Thomas P. Lewis
- tall plastic jar (olive jar)
- tray or baking pan with sides
- aluminum foil
- baking soda
- vinegar
- red food coloring (optional)

Procedure

1. Read a book about how volcanoes are formed and how they erupt.
2. Put the jar in the center of the tray.
3. Tuck the ends of the aluminum foil inside the jar opening. Use the foil to make a volcano shape around the jar. Keep the foil on the tray.
4. Put ¼ cup (57 g) of baking soda in the jar.
5. Add a few drops of red food coloring, if desired.
6. Discuss what happens when a real volcano erupts and how the magma comes up out of the hole and down the sides of the volcano.
7. Pour ½ cup (120 mL) of vinegar into the jar.

Art Activities for Vv

Violet Paintings

Materials
- 9" (23 cm) squares of construction paper (one per child)
- violet, light green, and yellow paint
- cotton swabs
- shallow cups

Preparation: Pour the paint into shallow cups.

Procedure
1. Paint violets by putting five dots of violet paint in a circle for each flower.
2. When dry, add a yellow dot in the center.
3. Paint stems and rounded leaves with light green paint.

Vegetable Vests

Materials
- brown paper grocery bags
- vegetable patterns (page 225)
- old magazines or seed catalogs
- crayons or markers
- scissors
- glue

Preparation: Cut out pictures of veggies from magazines or seed catalogs. Duplicate the vegetable patterns for each child.

Procedure
1. Cut up the center of the paper bag. Cut holes for the neck from the bottom and holes for the arms from the sides of the bag.
2. Color the vegetables.
3. Cut out the vegetables and glue them on the vests.

(**Optional:** Have a vegetable treat and sing "The Veggie Song" on page 226.)

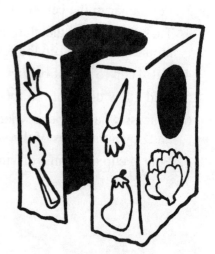

Valentines

Materials
- 9" x 12" (23 cm x 30 cm) sheets of construction paper (one per child)
- old magazines
- scissors
- glue
- crayons or markers

Procedure
1. Fold the construction paper in half.
2. Fold the front side in half again.
3. Cut a heart out of the paper, starting at the fold.
4. Glue a picture inside the card so that it can be seen through the heart.
5. Write "Be My Valentine" on the front of the card.
6. Decorate the cards with crayons or markers.

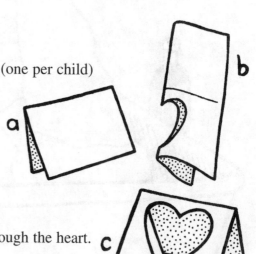

Vegetable Vests

Vegetable Patterns
Each student will need one copy of this page.

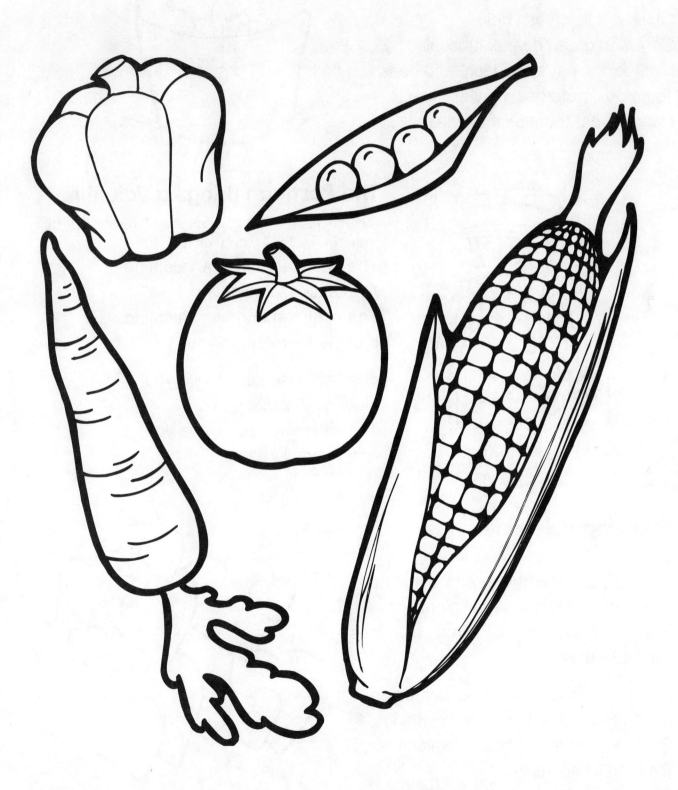

Songs and Fingerplays for Vv

The Veggie Song

(Sing to the tune of "Twinkle, Twinkle, Little Star.")
Carrots, celery, peppers, too,
I love veggies, yes I do!
Corn and green beans, broccoli,
Lettuce, cabbage, spinach, and peas
Tomatoes, potatoes, they are fine.
I want to eat them all the time.

The Postman Brings a Valentine

(Sing to the tune of "Mulberry Bush." Need a valentine with "I Love You" printed on it.)
The postman brings a valentine,
A valentine, a valentine,
The postman brings a valentine,
It came for me from you.

The valentine says I love you,
I love you, I love you
The valentine says I love you,
And I love you, too!

Counting Valentines

(Sing to the tune of "Ten Little Indians.")
One red, two red, three red valentines,
Four red, five red, six red valentines
Seven red, eight red, nine red valentines,
Ten red valentines.

Ten red, nine red, eight red valentines.
Seven red, six red, five red valentines,
Four red, three red, two red valentines,
One red valentine.

*(**Note:** Use a feltboard and ten red valentines to illustrate this song.)*

My Pocket Book for Vv

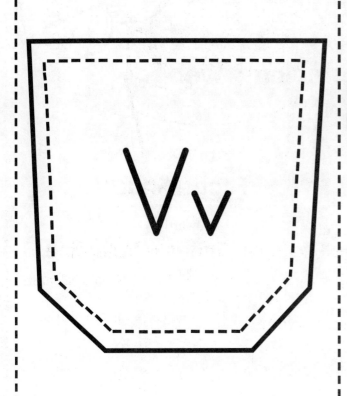

valentine

1

vet

2

We gave a valentine to the vet.

3

Ww

wall • watermelon • web

Story Books

I Went Walking by Sue Williams

I Wish I Had Duck Feet by Theo LeSieg

Mirette on the High Wire by Emily Arnold McCully

Mrs. Wishy Washy by Joy Cowley

Wacky Wednesday by Theo LeSieg

Wait Till the Moon Is Full by Margaret Wise Brown

Waiting for Wings by Lois Ehlert

What Is the World Made Of? by Kathleen Weidner Zoehfeld

Wiggling Worms at Work by Wendy Pfeffer

The Wind Blew by Pat Hutchins

Foods/Snacks

- waffles
- walnuts
- water
- watermelon
- wedges of cheese or fruit

Getting Started

1. Introduce the letter and the special picture. Read a book with the letter **W** in the title. Brainstorm a list of other words that begin with a **Ww** and write the words on a chart. Include the names of any children in the class whose names begin with **W**. (**Note:** When introducing the students to any of the activities or worksheets connected to the letter, the emphasis should be on the connection to the letter and the letter sound.)

2. Play the singing game, Go In and Out the Window. Have students form a circle and hold hands. Then have them raise their hands up in the air. One student will be chosen to be the leader. While all the students are singing, the leader will go in and out of the circle under the upraised hands. When the verse ends, the leader will choose another person to be his or her partner and take the hand of that person. Now, two students will go in and out of the circle. Then the leader will choose a new leader and the game continues.

Go In and Out the Window

Go in and out the window,

Go in and out the window.

Go in and out the window,

As we have done before.

Now stand and face your partner,

Now stand and face your partner.

Now stand and face your partner,

As we have done before.

Language Arts for Ww

Ww Wall of Words

Materials

- 4" x 9" (10 cm x 23 cm) rectangles of red paper
- large white index cards
- marker
- glue
- tape

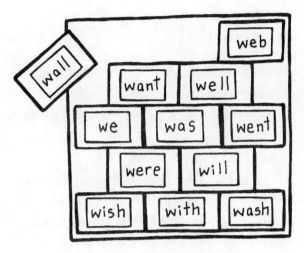

Procedure

1. Write words beginning with **Ww** in large printing on the white cards. (Some suggested words: *watermelon, wall, web, want, was, we, went, were, will, wish*, and *with*.)

2. Glue the white cards on the red paper to resemble bricks.

3. Tape the cards to a board or wall in a brick pattern.

4. Continue to build the wall by adding more **Ww** words.

Wishes

Materials

- *Wish for a Fish* by Bonnie Worth or *I Wish I Had Duck Feet* by Theo LeSieg
- chart paper and marker
- 12" x 18" (30 cm x 46 cm) sheets of construction paper (one per child)
- crayons or markers
- several pictures of things wished for

Procedure

1. Discuss things people wish for, and share pictures of wishes.

2. Read a book about wishes.

3. Use chart paper to make a word map about wishes.

4. Fold a piece of construction paper in thirds for each child. Write the numerals *1, 2,* and *3* (one at the top of each box).

5. In each box, the students draw a picture of something they wish for.

6. Display the pictures with the title, "My Three Wishes."

Language Arts for Ww *(cont.)*

Wagon Walk

Materials

- chart paper and marker
- worksheet (see below)
- crayons or markers

Preparation: Duplicate the worksheet below for each child.

Procedure

1. Have the students sit in a circle on the floor.
2. The teacher says, "I went for a walk with my wagon and on the way I saw a waterfall (or another word beginning with **Ww**).
3. The first student will have a turn and say, "I went for a walk with my wagon and on the way I saw a (word beginning with **Ww**) and a waterfall."
4. Go around the circle and have each student add a new word beginning with **Ww** and say all the words that have already been given.
5. Write the words on the chart paper. (Words could be *watch, windmill, water, whiskers,, web, wire, worm, window, word, waffle, walnut, witch,* and *wings*.)
6. Complete the worksheet by drawing something that begins with a **W** in the wagon. Color the picture.

I went for a walk with my wagon.

In the wagon there was a _____.

Name _____

Printing Practice for Ww

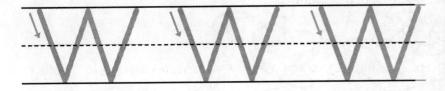

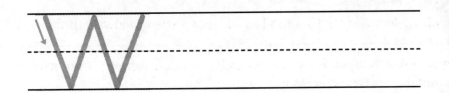

watermelon

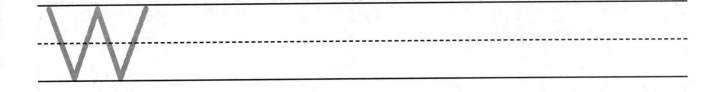

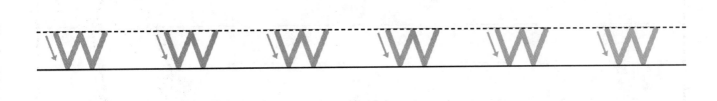

Name _____

Word Practice for Ww

watermelon

wall

web

I like watermelon.

Science Activities for Ww

Water Takes the Shape of the Container It Is In

Materials

- transparent containers of various sizes and shapes
- pitcher
- water
- measuring cups
- chart paper and marker

Preparation: When collecting transparent containers, try to find ones that look very different, but hold the same amount. Fill all the containers with 1 cup (240 mL) of water.

Procedure

1. Observe the containers of water with the students.
2. Ask students which containers have the most water.
3. Write students' responses on the chart.
4. Measure the water in each container and write the amount on the chart.
5. Discuss the fact that water looks different in each container because water takes the shape of the container it is in.

What Is the World Made Of?

Materials

- *What Is the World Made Of?* by Kathleen Weidner Zoehfeld
- three sheets of chart paper
- red, green, and blue markers
- sugar cubes
- water, some liquid and some frozen
- balloon
- shallow dish
- play dough
- rolling pin
- cookie cutter
- perfume spray

Preparation: At the top of the first chart, write the word, "Solid" in green; the word, "Liquid" in blue on the second chart; and the word "Gases" in red on the third chart.

Procedure

1. Brainstorm things that are solids, liquids, and gases.
2. Read the book and discuss that one example of a gas is perfume, one example of a liquid is water, and one example of a solid is play dough.
3. Roll out the play dough and use the cookie cutter to make a shape. The play dough keeps its shape.
4. Teach the students that some things can change from one category to another. Show ice cubes melting in the sun. Dissolve suger cubes in a glass of water. Blow air into a balloon.
5. Spray the liquid perfume in the air. We can smell it even if we can't see it because it is now a gas.
6. Show how water can change from liquid to a solid ice cube and then evaporate and become a gas. Put three ice cubes in a shallow dish. Watch the ice melt. Then watch the water disappear as it evaporates.

Art Activities for Ww

Wind Socks

Materials

- 12" x 18" (30 x 46 cm) sheets of light colored construction paper (one per child)
- crepe-paper streamers
- crayons or markers
- stapler
- paper punch
- string

Procedure

1. Decorate the construction paper with crayons or markers.
2. Roll the paper into a cylinder and staple it together.
3. Use the paper punch to punch four holes equal distances around the top.
4. Tie four strings, each 18" (46 cm) long, through the holes and then tie them together at the top.
5. Attach four crepe-paper streamers, each 24" (61 cm) long, equal distances around the bottom with a stapler.
6. Hang the wind socks where the wind will make them move.

We Went to Look Out the Window

Materials

- chart paper and marker
- crayons or markers
- 12" x 18" (30 cm x 46 cm) sheets of construction paper (one per child)
- 1" x 12" (3 cm x 30 cm) paper strips (two per child)
- 1" x 18" (3 cm x 46 cm) paper strips (two per child)
- old magazines or calendars
- glue

Procedure

1. Look out the window and see what you can see. Write what you see on the chart paper.
2. Find a picture in a magazine or a calendar, or draw a picture on the construction paper.
3. Glue it on the paper.
4. Add the paper strips to create a windowpane.
5. Display the new windows around the classroom.

Songs and Fingerplays for Ww

Wee Willie Winkie

(Traditional)
Wee Willie Winkie
Runs through the town
Upstairs and downstairs
In his nightgown.

Rapping at the windows
Crying through the lock,
"Are the children all in bed?
For now it's eight o'clock."

One Little, Two Little, Three Little Witches

(Sing to the tune of "Ten Little Indians.")
One little, two little, three little witches
(Hold up one, then two, then three fingers.)
Flying over haystacks, jumping over ditches.
(Make three fingers fly, then jump up and down.)
Slide down the moon without any hitches,
(Slide fingers down.)
Heigh-ho! Halloween!
(March for five steps.)

Let's Go Walking

Let's go walking,
Walking, walking,
(Walk in a circle.)
Let's go walking,
Far, far, away.
Let's walk back again,
Back again, back again,
(Turn around walk the other way.)
Let's walk back again,
Home the same day!

Songs and Fingerplays for Ww *(cont.)*

Here's a Little Washboard

(Traditional)

Here's a little washboard;

(Hold up palm of your left hand.)

Here's a little tub;

(Make a circle with fingers on your right hand.)

Here's a little cake of soap,

(Make an oval with fingers on the right hand.)

And here's the way we scrub.

(Have fingers go up and down on your left hand.)

Here's a line way up high;

(Draw an imaginary line in the air.)

Now the clothes are drying.

(Wave your fingers back and forth.)

Hear the wind come whistling by;

(Cup hand to your ear.)

See! The clothes are flying.

(Wave your hand harder.)

Variation: Read the book, *Mrs. Wishy Washy* by Joy Cowley, after learning this fingerplay.

My Pocket Book for Ww

watermelon 1

wall 2

The watermelon is by the wall. 3

Xx

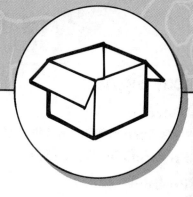

box • fox • six

Story Books

The Adventures of Taxi Dog by Debra and Sal Barracca

Can a Fox Wear Polka-Dotted Socks? by Janie Spaht Gill

Fox at School by Edward Marshall

Fox in Socks by Dr. Seuss

Hattie and the Fox by Mem Fox

Hello, Red Fox by Eric Carle

Ox-Cart Man by Donald Hall

Red Fox and His Canoe by Nathaniel Benchley

Rosie's Walk by Pat Hutchins

Six Dinner Sid by Inga Moore

Foods/Snacks

- brownie mix
- cake mix
- cereal mix
- cocoa mix
- cookie mix

Getting Started

1. Introduce the letter and the special picture. Read a book with the letter **X** in the title. Brainstorm a list of other words that begin with an **Xx** and write the words on a chart. Include the names of any children in the class whose names begin with **X**. (**Note:** When introducing the students to any of the activities or worksheets connected to the letter, the emphasis should be on the connection to the letter and the letter sound.)

2. Play a game of Run, Fox, Run. Go to the gym or playground where there is enough room to spread out and run. Divide the class into two groups. One group will be the "foxes," and the other group will be the "hounds." Decide on a home base and boundaries. The hounds stand behind home base. The foxes decide on a group leader. The foxes spread out and when they are ready, the leader yells, "Run, foxes, run!" The hounds try to catch the foxes before they can get back to home base. The foxes that are caught become hounds for the next game until all or most of the foxes are caught. Start over, with the foxes and hounds switching roles.

Language Arts for Xx

Exit Signs

Materials

- large piece of red paper

Preparation: Write the word, "EXIT," in large lettering on the red paper.

Procedure

1. Teach the students to read the word, "EXIT."
2. Show the sign and spell the word several times aloud.
3. Discuss the importance of knowing where the exit signs are in case of a fire or other emergency.
4. Go for a walk around the school and point out exit signs.

Snack Mix

Materials

- permanent marker
- large bowl and spoon
- 10 cups (2400 mL) square and circle shaped cereal
- bag of chocolate chips
- bag of nuts
- bag of banana chips
- small plastic resealable bags (one per child)

Preparation: Check for food allergies bafore starting activity. Using a permanent marker, write the word *mix* on each plastic bag.

Procedure

1. Pour all the cereal, chips, and nuts in the large mixing bowl.
2. Stir gently while singing "The Mixing Song" (page 245).
3. Put ½ cup (120 mL) of the mix in each of the plastic bags. Save for snack time.

X's and O's

Materials

- paper plates (5 per pair of students)
- craft sticks (10 per pair of students)
- glue and scissors
- sidewalk chalk or masking tape

Procedure

1. Teach the students to play the game, Tic Tac Toe, on the chalkboard.
2. Cut the center out of the paper plates to make rings (**O**'s).
3. Put a drop of glue in the center of a craft stick and put another craft stick on top, crosswise, to make an **X**. Each pair of students will need five **O**'s and five **X**'s.
4. Go outside to a safe place where a large Tic Tac Toe game can be drawn on the sidewalk using sidewalk chalk. This game could also be played inside using masking tape on the floor.

Name _____

Printing Practice for Xx

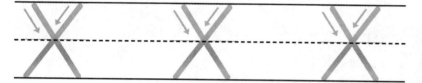

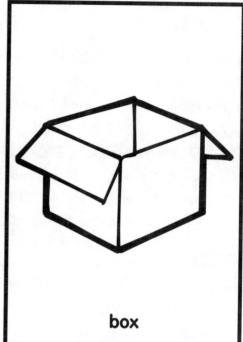

box

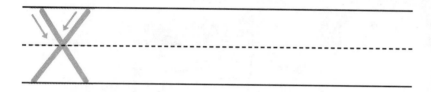

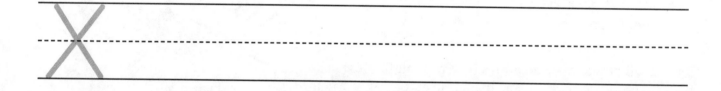

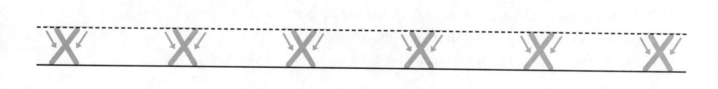

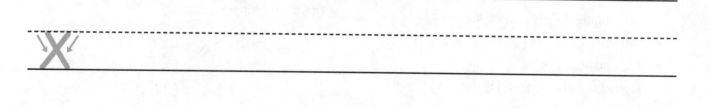

Word Practice for Xx

box

fox

six

A fox is in a box.

Science and Art Activity for Xx

Xx Is for X-Ray Machine

Materials

- 2 small pudding cups for each machine
- 11" tall (28 cm) cereal box (one per student or group)
- skeleton and person patterns (pages 243–244)
- black acrylic paint or black paper
- paintbrushes
- clear cellophane or kitchen wrap
- glue
- tape
- crayons or markers
- scissors
- pictures and small objects that end with **x**

Preparation: Duplicate the skeleton and person patterns for each child. Cut the top off the cereal boxes. On the front of each box, cut out a large rectangular shape without cutting through to the edges.

Procedure

1. Paint the inside and the outside of the box with black acrylic paint (or cover it with black paper). Allow time for the box to dry.

2. Color and cut out the skeleton and person patterns.

3. Glue the skeleton inside the cereal box (against the back) so that it can be seen through the hole in the front of the box.

4. Tape a piece of cellophane inside the box (against the front) to cover the hole in the front. This will be the X-Ray Machine window.

5. Glue the head piece (Tab A) to the top of the back of the box, so that it appears someone is behind the box.

6. Glue the arm pieces (Tab B) to the back edges of the box so that the arms stick out.

7. To make the leg stands for the X-Ray Machine, glue one pudding cup on each end of the bottom of the cereal box.

8. Glue the feet (Tab C) to the bottom back of the box. You will be able to see the feet between the pudding cups.

9. Fill the container with small objects and picture cutouts of things that end with the letter **x**.

Xx Is for X-Ray Machine

Skeleton Pattern

Each student or group will need one copy of this page.

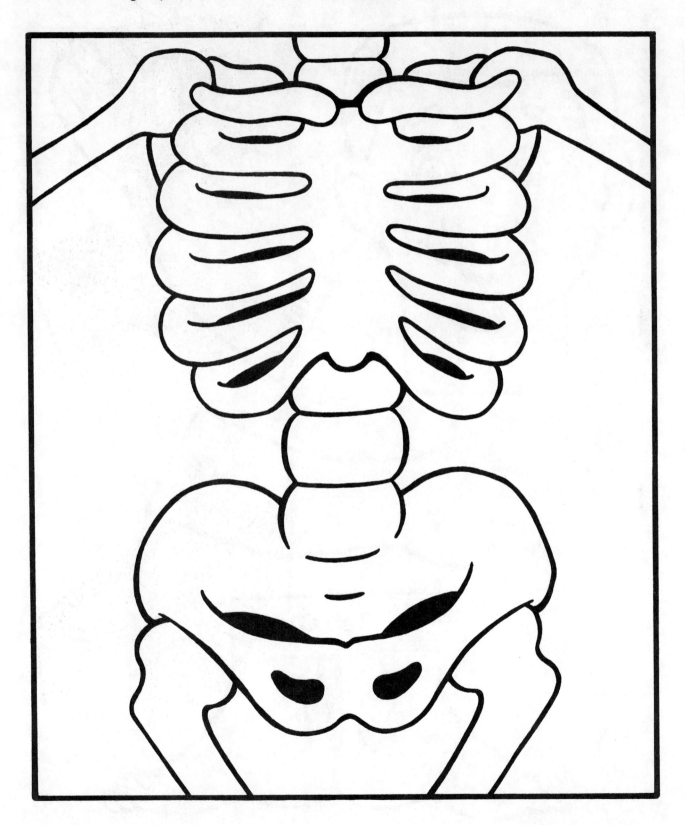

Xx Is for X-Ray Machine *(cont.)*

Person Pattern

Each student will need one copy of this page.

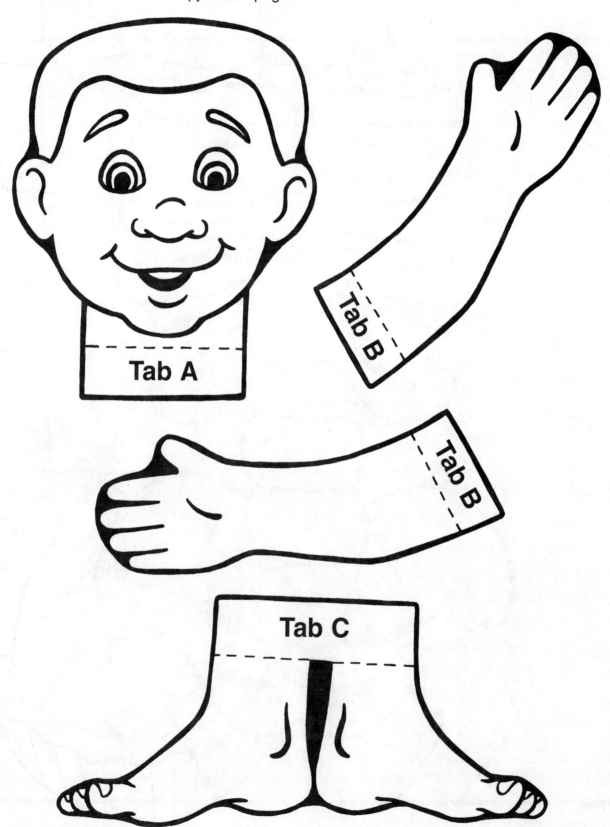

Tab A

Tab B

Tab B

Tab C

Songs and Fingerplays for Xx

The Box Song

(*Sing to the tune of "Twinkle, Twinkle, Little Star."*)

We like boxes, yes we do
Tall ones, short ones,
Square boxes, too.
We can use them for a store
Look around and get some more.
We like boxes, yes we do
Tall ones, short ones,
Square boxes, too.

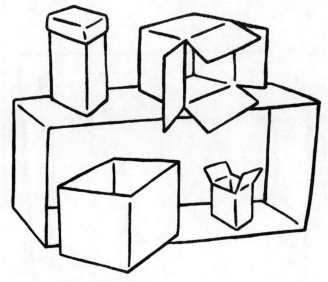

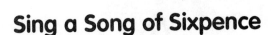

The Mixing Song

(*Sing to the tune of "Row, Row, Row Your Boat."*)

Mix, mix, mix your dough
Mix it all together,
Mix, mix, mix, mix
Mix it all together.

Sing a Song of Sixpence

(*Traditional*)

Sing a song of sixpence
A pocket full of rye
Four and twenty blackbirds baked in a pie
When the pie was opened
The birds began to sing,
Now wasn't that a dainty dish
To set before the king?
The king was in the counting house
Counting out his money
The queen was in the parlor
Eating bread and honey
The maid was in the garden,
Hanging out the clothes
Along came a blackbird
And snipped off her nose!

My Pocket Book for Xx

Xx

fox

1

box

2

The fox is in a box.

3

Yy

yard • yarn • yes

Story Books

Is It Red? Is It Yellow? Is It Blue? by Tana Hoban

Little Blue and Little Yellow by Leo Lionni

Marco's Colors: Red, Yellow, Blue by Tomie dePaola

Red, Blue, Yellow Shoe by Tana Hoban

Why I Sneeze, Shiver, Hiccup, and Yawn by Melvin Berger

Yertle the Turtle and Other Stories by Dr. Seuss

Young Larry by Jill Pinkwater

Yucky Reptile Alphabet Book by Jerry Pallotta

Yummers! by James Marshall

Yummers Too! by James Marshall

Foods/Snacks

- yams
- yeast bread
- yellow foods—banana, lemon, corn, butterscotch
- yellow gelatin
- yogurt
- yummy pudding

Getting Started

1. Introduce the letter and the special picture. Read a book with the letter **Y** in the title. Brainstorm a list of other words that begin with a **Yy** and write the words on a chart. Include the names of any children in the class whose names begin with **Y**. (**Note:** When introducing the students to any of the activities or worksheets connected to the letter, the emphasis should be on the connection to the letter and the letter sound.)

2. Make flags and have a parade while singing "Yankee Doodle." Look at pictures of flags and let students design their own flags or choose one to copy. Draw and color flags on a 9" x 12" (23 cm x 30 cm) sheet of construction paper. Tape the flag to a ruler or large straw. Play a tape or CD and sing "Yankee Doodle" while marching. Choose one student to be the leader. Then have that student choose the next leader.

Language Arts for Yy

Yes and No

Materials

- index cards (two per child)
- list of questions to ask students
- markers

Preparation: Write the word *yes* on half of the index cards. Write the word *no* on the other half. Give each student two cards, one with *yes* on it and one with *no* on it. Create a list of questions to ask the students. Examples are given below:

- Do you like to go to gym?
- Can you tie your shoes?
- Do you like to play with blocks?
- Do you like to go to the zoo?
- Can you button your shirt?
- Do you like to eat spaghetti?
- Do you think it would be fun to have an elephant for a pet?
- Do you think you would like to ride on a motorcycle?

Procedure

1. Teach the students to read and spell the words *yes* and *no*.
2. Ask the questions (see samples above) and have the students hold up the card with the correct answer.

Yellow Book

Materials

- *Is It Red? Is It Yellow? Is It Blue?* by Tana Hoban or *Red, Blue, Yellow Shoe* by Tana Hoban
- 12" x 18" (30 cm x 46 cm) sheets of white construction paper (one per child)
- yellow paint
- paintbrushes
- 3 sheets of chart paper and marker
- stapler, rings, or comb binder

Procedure

1. Ask students to think of something yellow.
2. Read a book about the primary colors.
3. At the top of the first chart, write the word *red*, write *yellow* on the second chart, and *blue* on the third chart. Brainstorm things that are these colors.
4. Each student paints a picture using yellow paint.
5. When the painting is dry, write the word telling what the object is at the bottom of the page and assemble into a book.
6. Add a cover with the title, "Our Yellow Book."

Name _____

Printing Practice for Yy

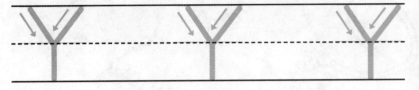

yarn

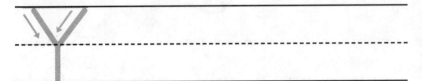

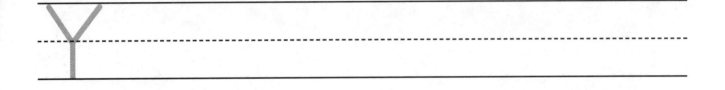

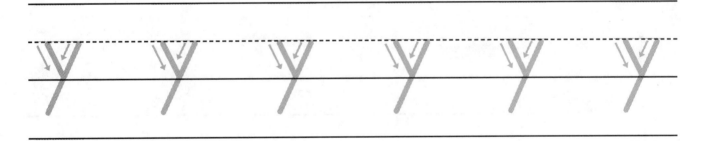

Name _____

Word Practice for Yy

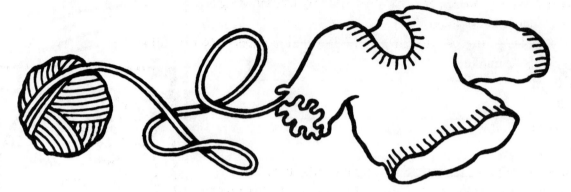

yarn

yard

yes

I see the yarn.

Science Activities for Yy

Yawn Manners

Materials

- *Why I Sneeze, Shiver, Hiccup, and Yawn* by Melvin Berger
- chart paper and marker
- 9" x 12" (23 cm x 30 cm) sheets of construction paper (one per child)
- crayons or markers
- tissues
- glue
- scissors

Procedure

1. Ask students if they know why people sneeze, shiver, hiccup, and yawn. Write their responses on the chart paper.
2. Read the book and discuss reflex actions.
3. Discuss when it is important to cover their mouths.
4. On the paper, have the students draw a large oval for the head, eyes, and nose, and a big round mouth yawning.
5. Trace and cut out one hand for each student.
6. Glue the hand over the mouth.
   Display with the pictures with the title, "Cover Your Yawn."

Yeast Experiment

Find out what makes bread have little air holes.

Materials

- 2 slices of bread
- recipe for bread, which includes yeast
- 2 glass measuring cups, 2 cups (475 mL) capacity
- cold water
- 2 tablespoons (30 mL) granulated sugar
- two bowls
- oven or bread maker (optional)
- 2 packages of active dry yeast
- warm water, 110°F (43°C)

Procedure

1. Pose the question, "Why does bread have air holes?"
2. Flatten one of the bread slices with the palm of your hand.
3. Examine the two slices of bread. What do you observe?
4. Look at the recipe for bread. What is yeast? (The ingredient that makes dough rise.)
5. Put a package of active dry yeast and 2 tablespoons (30 mL) of granulated sugar in each bowl. Add 1 cup (240 mL) of water to each bowl—warm water in one bowl and cold water in the other. Observe the yeast in the warm water. It will bubble as it grows.
6. Discuss, "Why does bread have to be kept warm when it is being made?"
7. If possible, bake bread with your students.

Art Activities for Yy

Yellow Yarn Art

Materials

- yellow yarn
- disposable plastic plates (one per child)
- scissors
- tape

Procedure

1. Using scissors, snip into the edges of the plate.
2. Tape the end of the yarn to the bottom of the plate.
3. Wind the yarn across the plate and into the slits, and around the back and across the top again.
4. Keep going until the end of the yarn. Tape the end to the back of the plate.
5. Display the plates with the title, "Yellow Yarn Art."

Yellow Crayon Resist Pictures

Materials

- 12" x 18" (30 cm x 46 cm) sheets of white construction paper (one per child)
- wax crayons
- yellow paint
- shallow dishes
- large paintbrushes

Preparation: Pour the paint into the dishes. Thin the paint with water.

Procedure

1. Use the wax crayons to color a picture. Press hard on the crayons to leave more wax than usual on the paper.
2. Use the large brush with the yellow paint to paint lightly in long strokes over the entire paper.
3. When the pictures are dry, display with the title, "Yellow, Yellow."

Yellow Raincoat Mural

Materials

- raincoat pattern (page 253)
- mural paper
- crayons or markers
- scissors
- glue

Preparation: Duplicate the raincoat for each child.

Procedure

1. Color the raincoats yellow. Cut out the patterns and glue them on the mural paper.
2. Use crayons or markers to add heads, hands, and feet to the raincoats. Make blue dots for rain.
3. Display the mural with the title, "We Love Our Yellow Raincoats."

Yellow Raincoat Mural

Raincoat Pattern

Each student will need one copy of this page.

Songs and Fingerplays for Yy

Love Somebody

(*Traditional*)

Love somebody, yes, I do

(*Stand in a circle.*)

Love somebody, yes, I do

(*One student goes to the center of the circle.*)

Love somebody, yes I do

(*Turn around slowly.*)

I love somebody

(*Student in center points to one student.*)

And it must be YOU!

(*That student goes to the center.*)

You Are Special

(*Sing to the tune of "Where is Thumbkin?"*)

You are special,
You are special.
Yes, you are,
Yes, you are.
You're a good friend too,
That is why I like you,
Yes, that's true
Yes, that's true.

Yankee Doodle

(*Traditional*)

Yankee Doodle went to town
Riding on a pony.
Stuck a feather in his cap
And called it macaroni.
Yankee Doodle keep it up
Yankee Doodle dandy.
Mind the music and the step
And with the girls be handy.

My Pocket Book for Yy

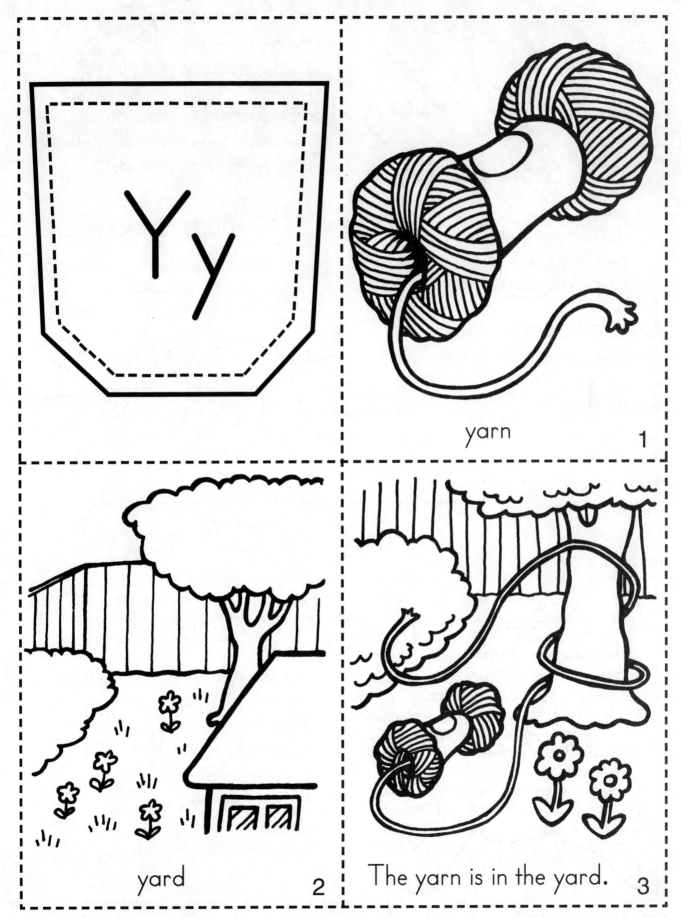

yarn 1

yard 2

The yarn is in the yard. 3

Zz

zebra • zipper • zoo

Story Books

African Animals ABC by Sarah L. Schuette
Children's Zoo by Tana Hoban
The Happy Lion by Louise Fatio
If I Ran the Zoo by Dr. Seuss
Mrs. Toggle's Zipper by Robin Pulver
My Visit to the Zoo by Aliki
1, 2, 3 to the Zoo by Eric Carle
Put Me in the Zoo by Robert Lopshire
Zoo by Gail Gibbons
Zoo-Looking by Mem Fox

Foods/Snacks

- cookies in **Z** shape
- ziti pasta
- zoo animal crackers
- zucchini
- zucchini bread

Getting Started

1. Introduce the letter and the special picture. Read a book with the letter **Z** in the title. Brainstorm a list of other words that begin with a **Zz** and write the words on a chart. Include the names of any children in the class whose names begin with **Z**. (**Note:** When introducing the students to any of the activities or worksheets connected to the letter, the emphasis should be on the connection to the letter and the letter sound.)

2. Play a game of Zoo Animal Charades. Students sit in a circle on the floor. Ask the students to think of a zoo animal they would like to imitate. (They should think of what actions the animal would do.) Choose one student to stand in the center of the circle and imitate the animal he or she chose. After imitating the animal, the student will choose another student who will guess the name of the animal. If the animal is guessed correctly, then that student will stand in the center and imitate a different animal. After three incorrect guesses, the student in the center will tell the class what the animal was and choose another student to be in the center.

Language Arts for Zz

Zipper Book

Materials

- zippers (one per child)
- 9" x 12" (23 cm x 30 cm) sheets of white construction paper or card stock (one per child)
- glue
- crayons or markers
- stapler, rings, or comb binder

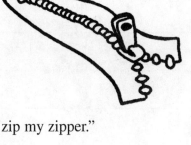

Preparation: On each sheet of paper, write the words, "I can zip my zipper."

Procedure

1. Close the zipper. Carefully put a line of glue down the cloth sides of the zipper.
2. Put the zipper in the center of the paper and let the glue dry.
3. Using crayons or markers, draw objects that have zippers, such as jackets, pants, shirts, tent flaps, purses, and suitcases.
4. Put the pages together in a book with a cover page, titled "Our Zipper Book."
5. Read the book as a class and have each student pull the zipper tab up and down as that student reads the page and tells about her or his pictures.

Zoo Visit

Materials

- *My Visit to the Zoo* by Aliki
- sheets of white construction paper (one per child)
- zoo video
- chart paper and marker
- crayons or markers
- zoo visit (optional)

Preparation: On each sheet of paper, write the sentence starter "At the zoo, I saw a _____."

Procedure

1. Read a book about the zoo.
2. View a video about the zoo or visit the zoo.
3. Brainstorm what the students saw and write the ideas on the chart paper.
4. Give each student a paper with the sentence starter, and help the students fill in the sentence to tell what they saw.
5. Draw a picture to illustrate the sentence. Display the pictures with the title, "A Visit to the Zoo."

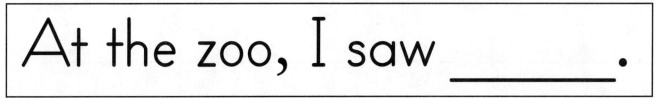

At the zoo, I saw _____.

Name _____

Printing Practice for Zz

zebra

Name _____

Word Practice for Zz

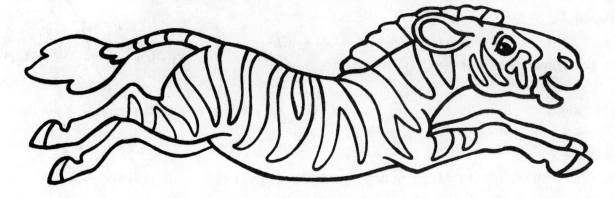

zebra

zipper

zoo

I see the zebra.

Science Activity for Zz

Zoo Animals

Use animal riddles to help teach the characteristics of zoo animals.

Materials
- 5" x 8" (13 cm x 20 cm) index cards
- zoo animal patterns (page 261)
- marker
- glue
- copy of riddles (below)

Preparation: Duplicate the zoo animal patterns. Glue each animal on an index card. Cut out the riddles and glue each one to the back of the appropriate card.

Procedure
1. Read each riddle aloud. Have students choose the right picture for the description.
2. Place a set of cards in the science center for an independent activity.

I can be brown, black, or white.
I live in a den and my babies are
called cubs.
I am a _____ .

I am the largest land animal.
I have big ears and a long trunk.
I am an _____ .

I am the tallest land animal.
I have brown spots and a very
long neck.
I am a _____ .

I have fur, big teeth, and a very
loud roar.
If I am a male, I have a big mane.
I am a _____ .

I have a very long tail.
I can jump from branch to branch.
I am a _____ .

I live in the water and make a
noise like a "bark."
I eat fish and have flippers.
I am a _____ .

I have four legs and big teeth.
I look like a cat and have stripes.
I am a _____ .

I have four legs and look
like a horse.
I have black and white stripes.
I am a _____ .

Zoo Animals

Zoo Animal Patterns

Make one copy of this page for a class set.

Art Activities for Zz

Zebra Puppets

Materials

- zebra pattern (page 263)
- white paper lunch bags
- black crayons
- glue
- scissors

Preparation: Duplicate the zebra pattern for each child.

Procedure

1. Use the scissors to cut out the zebra's head and tail.
2. Glue the head on the bottom of the white bag so the fold is in the front.
3. Decorate the bag with black stripes to show the body of the zebra.
4. Attacht the tail.
5. Hold the puppet and sing songs about the zoo (see page 264).

Shoebox Zoo

Materials

- shoebox (one per child)
- old magazines or calendars featuring zoo animals
- scissors
- glue
- ⅓" x 9" (1 cm x 23 cm) black paper strips (eight per child)
- paper, to cover the sides of the shoeboxes

Preparation: Cut out pictures of zoo animals from old magazines or print out zoo pictures from the computer.

Procedure

1. Glue the animal pictures inside each shoebox.
2. Cover the outside of the box with paper.
3. Put a drop of glue on the ends of the black paper strips and evenly space them. Glue the strips over the opening on the box to resemble bars on a cage.
4. Display the boxes with the title, "Our Shoebox Zoo."

Zebra Puppets

Zebra Pattern

Each child will need one copy of this page.

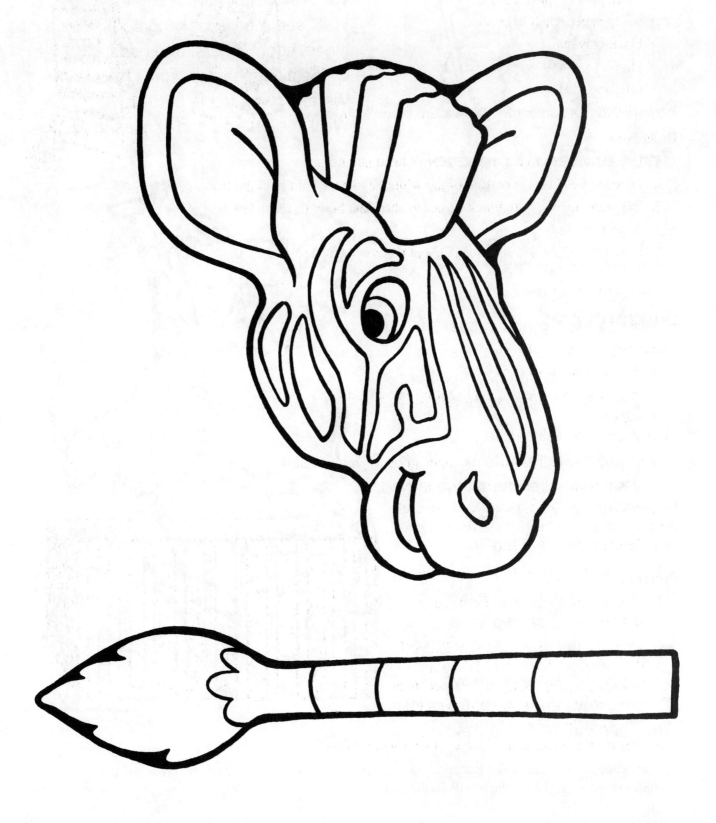

Songs and Fingerplays for Zz

We Are Going to the Zoo

(Sing to the tune of "Twinkle, Twinkle, Little Star.")
We are going to the zoo.
We'll see monkeys, kangaroos,
Lions, tigers, bears, and birds,
Camels, elephants, zebras, too.
We are going to the zoo.
We'll see chimps and snakes there, too.

The Children at the Zoo

(Sing to the tune of "The Farmer in the Dell.")
The children at the zoo
The children at the zoo
They want to see the animals
The children at the zoo.

They see the big brown bear
They see the big brown bear
They see him eating big meatballs
They see the big brown bear.

They see the tall giraffe
They see the tall giraffe
They see him chewing on the leaves
They see the tall giraffe.

They see the great big lion
They see the great big lion
The lion eats a lot of meat
They see the great big lion.

They see the funny monkeys
They see the funny monkeys
The monkeys eat a lot of fruit
They see the funny monkeys.

Variation: Have the students stand in a circle. Two or three students can stand in the center, making the motions for the words to the song.

My Pocket Book for Zz

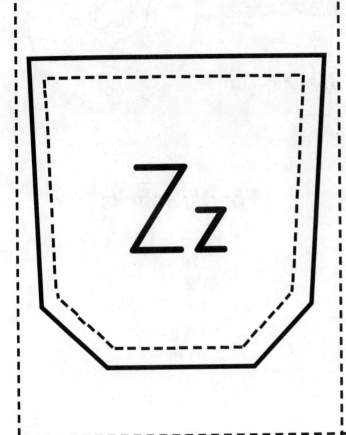

zebra 1

zoo 2

The zebra is at the zoo. 3

Ch

chair • chick • chill

Story Books

A Chair for My Mother by Vera B. Williams

Changes, Changes by Pat Hutchins

Cherries and Cherry Pits by Vera B. Williams

Chicka, Chicka, Boom, Boom by Bill Martin, Jr.

Chicken Chuck by Bill Martin, Jr.

Chicken Little by Steven Kellogg

A Chocolate Moose for Dinner by Fred Gwynne

Curious George Goes to a Chocolate Factory by H. A. Rey

Peter's Chair by Ezra Jack Keats

The Seven Chinese Brothers by Margaret Mahy

The Seven Chinese Sisters by Kathy Tucker

Foods/Snacks

- cherries
- cheese
- cheesecake
- Chinese noodles
- chips and dip
- chocolate

Getting Started

1. Introduce the letter and the special picture. Read a book with the letter **Ch** in the title. Brainstorm a list of other words that begin with a **Ch** and write the words on a chart. Include the names of any children in the class whose names begin with **Ch**. (**Note:** When introducing the students to any of the activities or worksheets connected to the letter, the emphasis should be on the connection to the letter and the letter sound.)

2. Play a game of Musical Chairs. Put chairs, one less than the number of students, in two rows back to back. Have the students stand in a row behind the chairs. Play music. When you stop the music, the students will sit down in a chair. Remind the students to walk and carefully sit down without pushing anyone else. Students who do not find a chair are "out" and will sit together. Remove one chair after each round and continue until one student is left.

#3380 Getting Ready to Read   266   ©Teacher Created Resources, Inc.

Language Arts for Ch

Chester the Chick

Write a class story about a chick named Chester.

Materials

- version of *Chicken Little*
- toy chick or picture of a chick
- chart paper and marker
- scissors
- glue
- 12" x 18" (30 cm x 46 cm) sheets of construction paper
- stapler or rings and hole punch

Procedure

1. Show students a toy chick or a picture of a chick.

2. Brainstorm what the students think about the things a young chick named Chester might do that begins with the digraph **Ch**. For instance, draw with chalk, sit on a chair, eat chocolate, visit China, chat with a friend, pick cherries, or play checkers. Write the ideas on a word map.

3. When finished with the word map, read a story book about chicks.

4. Gather students in a group. Have students tell a complete sentence using ideas taken from the word map.

5. Write the sentences on chart paper while saying the words aloud.

6. Cut the sentence strips apart and glue them at the bottom of sheets of construction paper.

7. Students can illustrate these sentences individually or in pairs.

8. When finished, put the sheets together in a book with the title, "A Chick Named Chester." Reread several times and add the book to your classroom library.

chick

Name _____

Printing Practice for Ch

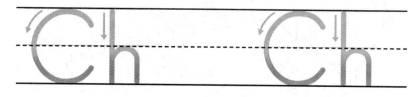

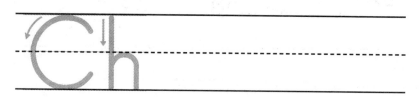

chick

Name _____

Word Practice for Ch

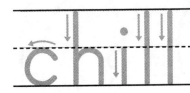

I see a chick.

Science Activity for Ch

Chimpanzees

Learn about chimpanzees, one of the endangered species.

Materials

- *The Chimpanzee* by Martin Banks or *To Be a Chimpanzee* by Chris and Martin Kratt
- chart paper and marker
- chimpanzee mask (see below)
- string
- crayons
- bananas
- scissors
- brown construction paper

Preparation: Duplicate the chimpanzee mask on brown paper for each child.

Procedure

1. Read a nonfiction book about chimpanzees.
2. List facts about chimpanzees on the chart
3. Make masks and add strings to tie them on.
4. Reread facts and dramatize a community of chimpanzees while eating bananas.

Chimpanzee Mask

Art Activities for Ch

Chalk Drawings

Materials

- chalk
- sheets of dark construction paper
- hair spray

Procedure

1. Review the class list of words beginning with **Ch**.

2. Demonstrate use of chalk and have students choose a word beginning with the **Ch** digraph to illustrate. Suggested drawings:

• chain	• cheese	• chicken	• chin
• chair	• cheetah	• children	• chips
• chalk	• cherries	• chill (chilly day)	• chocolate
• charcoal	• chick	• chimpanzee	• chop

3. When the chalk drawings are complete, spray them with hair spray to protect them.

4. Label the pictures. Display with the title, "**Ch** Words with Chalk."

Art Activities for Ch *(cont.)*

Chains of Paper

Materials
- chain patterns (page 273)
- scissors
- glue

Preparation: Duplicate the chain pattern page for each child.

Procedure
1. Review words that begin with **Ch**.
2. Cut out the paper strips on the dashed lines.
3. Make a loop with the first paper strip and glue the ends together, making sure the word is facing out.
4. Take the next strip, put it through the loop, and glue these ends together, making sure the word is facing out.
5. Repeat until all of the strips have been attached.
6. Hang the chains around the room.

Houses with Chimneys

Materials
- sheets of white construction paper (one per child)
- small squares of red construction paper (one per child)
- crayons
- glue

Procedure
1. Draw a house. (Teachers may need to model this for students.)
2. Glue a chimney (the red paper square) on top of the house.
3. Add lines to show bricks on the chimney.
4. Decorate the houses. Add a cherry tree to the yard.
5. Display pictures with the title, "Houses with Chimneys" and sing the song below.

See My Chimney

(Sing to the tune of "Frere Jacques.")
See my chimney,
See my chimney,
See the smoke,
See the smoke.
All the smoke is blowing out,
We will hear the people shout,
"See the smoke. See the smoke."

Chains of Paper

chain	chain
chair	chair
chalk	chalk
charcoal	charcoal
cheese	cheese
cheetah	cheetah
cherries	cherries
chick	chick
chicken	chicken
children	children
chill	chill
chimpanzee	chimpanzee
chin	chin
chips	chips
chocolate	chocolate
chop	chop

Songs and Fingerplays for Ch

Five Little Chickens

(*Traditional*)

Five little chickens standing in a row,

They nod their heads to the children, so.

They run to the left, they run to the right,

They stand up and stretch in the bright sunlight.

Along comes a dog, who's in for some fun.

"Cluck, cluck, cluck," see those five chickens run!

Chicks and Bugs

(*Traditional*)

Five little chickens by the old barn door;
One chased a beetle and then there were four.

Four little chickens under a tree;
One chased an ant and then there were three.

Three little chickens looked for something new;
One saw a grasshopper and then there were two.

Two little chickens said, "Oh, what fun!"
One saw a ladybug and then there was one.

One little chicken began to run;
For he saw a bee—then there were none!

Note: To use this as a feltboard story, you will need to make five little chicks, a barn door piece of construction paper, beetle, ant, grasshopper, ladybug, and a bee.

My Pocket Book for Ch

Ch

chick 1

chair 2

The chick sat on a chair. 3

Sh

sheep • ship • shop

Story Books

Bear Shadow by Frank Asch

George Shrinks by William Joyce

Shadow by Marcia Brown

Shapes, Shapes, Shapes by Tana Hoban

Sharks by Gail Gibbons

Sheep in a Jeep by Nancy Shaw

Sheep in a Shop by Nancy Shaw

Shortcut by Donald Crews

Show and Tell Day by Anne Rockwell

What Lives in a Shell? by Kathleen Weidner Zoehfeld

Foods/Snacks

- milk shakes
- shape cookies
- shell macaroni
- sherbet
- shredded wheat cereal

Getting Started

1. Introduce the letter and the special picture. Read a book with the letter **Sh** in the title. Brainstorm a list of other words that begin with an **Sh** and write the words on a chart. Include the names of any children in the class whose names begin with **Sh**. (**Note:** When introducing the students to any of the activities or worksheets connected to the letter, the emphasis should be on the connection to the letter and the letter sound.)

2. Look at shadows and watch what happens to the shadows when people move. Play Shadow Tag outside on a bright sunny day. Choose one student to be "It." The rest of the students will scatter and run to keep away from the person who is It. It tries to catch another person by stepping on her or his shadow. When It steps on another person's shadow, that person becomes It.
(**Management Tip:** Shadows are longer earlier and later in the day.)

Language Arts for Sh

Shape Names

Materials

- *Shapes, Shapes, Shapes* by Tana Hoban or *The Shape of Things* by Dayle Ann Dodds
- index cards
- objects, to sort by shape
- paper shapes cut from colored paper (several per child)
- sheets of construction paper (one per child)
- glue

Preparation: Write each of the following words on an index card: *circle, square, rectangle, triangle,* and *oval.*

Procedure

1. Read the book, *Shapes, Shapes, Shapes,* and discuss the objects on each page.
2. Introduce the students to the five shape words.
3. Hold up each object and match it to the appropriate shape word card. Sort all the objects by shape.
4. Distribute paper and an assortment of paper shapes to each student.
5. Try different designs before using the glue.
6. Glue the shapes on the paper.
7. Display the shape pictures with the shape name cards.

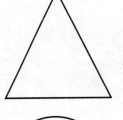

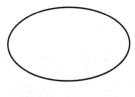

Shadows

Materials

- *Shadow* by Marcia Brown and *Hand Shadows* by Henry Bursill
- projector

Procedure

1. Discuss shadows and the fact that in order to see a shadow, there needs to be a bright light coming from one direction.
2. Read the book, *Shadow.*
3. Turn on the projector and make hand shadows. Use the book, *Hand Shadows* for suggestions.

Name _____

Printing Practice for Sh

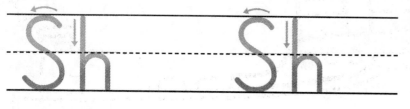

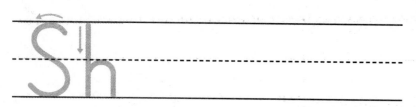

ship

Word Practice for Sh

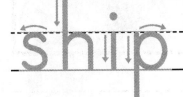

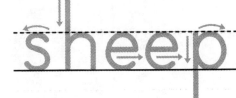

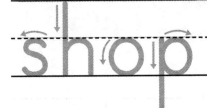

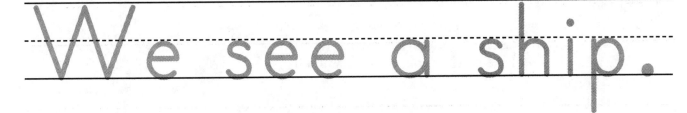

Science Activities for Sh

Shadow of the Sun

Materials

- bright sunny day
- 12" (30 cm) dowels or sticks
- craft dough
- chalk

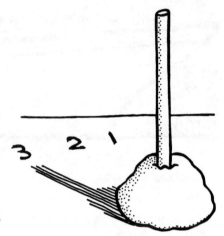

Procedure

1. Give each student a lump of craft dough and a stick.
2. Go outside in the morning to a spot where the sticks will not be disturbed. Put the dough on the ground and put the stick into the dough so that it stands upright.
3. Use the chalk to trace the shadow of the stick.
4. Write the numeral 1 next to the shadow.
5. Return at noon, and again in the afternoon, to trace the shadows and write 2 and 3 next to the appropriate lines.
6. Discuss observations.

Shells

Materials

- *What Lives in a Shell?* by Kathleen Weidner Zoehfeld and *A House for Hermit Crab* by Eric Carle
- chart paper and marker
- shells (bivalve and univalve)
- sheets of paper (one per pair or group of students)

Preparation: Fold paper in half and write "Univalve" at the top on one side, and "Bivalve" at the top on the other side.

Procedure

1. Read the book, *A House for Hermit Crab*.
2. Ask students what they already know about shells and write their responses on a word map.
3. Read the book, *What Lives in a Shell?*
4. Show shells and discuss the difference between a "univalve" shell and a "bivalve" shell. Univalves are circular (conch, murex) and bivalves have two matching sides (clamshells, mussels, scallops).

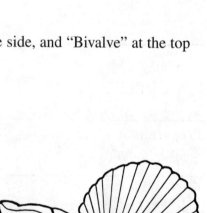

5. Give each pair or group of students a sheet for sorting shells into univalves and bivalves and a selection of shells.
6. Complete the lesson by adding new information to the word map.

*Suggestion: Ask your local fishmarket, restaurant, or butcher to save shells for you.

Art Activities for Sh

Shadow Silhouette Pictures

Materials

- projector
- tape
- 12" x 18" (30 cm x 46 cm) sheets of black paper (one per child)
- 12" x 18" (30 cm x 46 cm) sheets of white paper (one per child)
- scissors
- glue

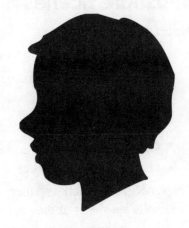

Procedure

1. Tape a large sheet of white paper on a wall.
2. Put a chair next to the paper and have the student sit on the chair so his or her profile is next to the paper.
3. Shine the light on the student and trace around the profile.
4. Remove the paper and lay on the black paper.
5. Cut the profile out of both sheets at one time.
6. Glue the black silhouette on the white construction paper.

Management Tip: While these portraits are time consuming and require the child to sit very still for a few minutes, they are a treasured memento. Be sure to write the name of each student and the date on the back of the portrait.

Sheep

Materials

- 5" x 8" (13 cm x 20 cm) index cards
  (one for each child, plus additional cards to cut the 3" ovals)
- cotton balls
- glue
- craft sticks
- crayons or markers

Preparation: Cut ovals from the index cards, about 3" (8 cm) long.

Procedure

1. Fold the index cards in half. The fold will be the top of the sheep.
2. Glue the oval for the head halfway inside the fold.
3. Draw an eye on either side of the oval.
4. Glue two craft sticks at the bottom of one side, and the other two at the bottom of the other side for the legs.
5. Put a little dab of glue on the side of the sheep and press a cotton ball into the glue. Continue until both sides are covered with cotton balls.

Variation: Cover small margarine tubs with cotton balls and use mini clothes pins for legs.

Art Activities for Sh *(cont.)*

Seashore Scenes

Materials

- 9" x 3" (23 cm x 8 cm) strips of sandpaper (one per child)
- 9" x 12" (23 cm x 30 cm) sheets of blue construction paper (one per child)
- shells
- glue
- crayons
- chart paper and marker

Preparation: On chart paper, write the tongue twister, "She sells seashells at the seashore."

Procedure

1. Read the tongue twister several times and invite students to say the sentence faster and faster.
2. Read the tongue twister slowly while pointing to the words.
3. Reassure students that you know it is difficult to say it quickly, but that is the point of a tongue twister.
4. Glue the strip of sandpaper to the bottom of the blue paper.
5. Glue the shells on the sandpaper.
6. Complete the picture with crayons.
7. Display the pictures with the tongue twister strip as a title.

Shadow Pictures

Materials

- sunny window
- large sheet of paper
- pencils
- objects to trace (toys)
- black paint
- paintbrushes

Preparation: On a large sheet of paper, write the title, "Our Shadow Pictures" using black paint.

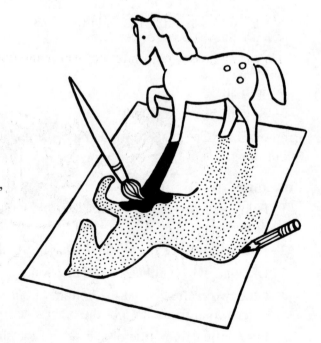

Procedure

1. Put the paper near a window where the sun will shine on it.
2. Place an object on the paper.
3. Trace around the shadow. (Some students may need help holding objects steadey while tracing).
4. Paint the shadow with black paint.
5. Display the pictures with the title, "Our Shadow Pictures."

Songs and Fingerplays for Sh

Shoo Fly
(Traditional)

Shoo fly, don't bother me,
Shoo fly, don't bother me.
Shoo fly, don't bother me,
For I belong to somebody.

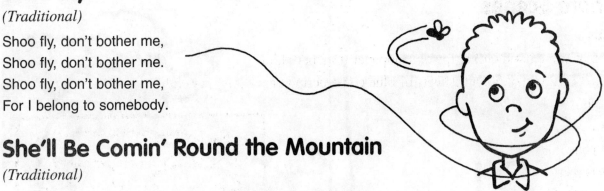

She'll Be Comin' Round the Mountain
(Traditional)

She'll be comin' round the mountain when she comes,
She'll be comin' round the mountain when she comes,
She'll be comin' round the mountain,
She'll be comin' round the mountain,
She'll be comin' round the mountain when she comes.

She'll be driving six white horses when she comes,
She'll be driving six white horses when she comes,
She'll be driving six white horses,
She'll be driving six white horses,
She'll be driving six white horses when she comes.

We will all go down to meet her when she comes, Hi, Babe!
We will all go down to meet her when she comes, Hi, Babe!
We will all go down to meet her,
We will all go down to meet her,
We will all go down to meet her when she comes, Hi, Babe!

My Pocket Book for Sh

Sh

sheep

1

ship

2

The sheep is on a ship.

3

Th

thimble • three • thumb

Story Books

Flash, Crash, Rumble, and Roll by Franklyn Branley
Goldilocks and the Three Bears by Jan Brett
Hand, Hand, Fingers, Thumb by Al Perkins
I Can Read about Thunder and Lightning by David Cutts
Thanksgiving Day by Gail Gibbons
Three Bears Holiday Rhyme Book by Jane Yolen
Three By the Sea by Edward Marshall
A Three Hat Day by Laura Geringer
Three Little Pigs by Patricia Siebert et al.
Three Little Pigs by Paul Galdone
Three Little Wolves and the Big Bad Pig by Helen Oxenbury
Thunder Cake by Patricia Polacco

Foods/Snacks

- thirteen chocolate chips
- three chocolate candies
- three jelly beans
- thumbprint cookies

Getting Started

1. Introduce the letter and the special picture. Read a book with the letter **Th** in the title. Brainstorm a list of other words that begin with a **Th** and write the words on a chart. Include the names of any children in the class whose names begin with **Th**. (**Note:** When introducing the students to any of the activities or worksheets connected to the letter, the emphasis should be on the connection to the letter and the letter sound.)

2. Read one of the many versions of *The Three Bears*, or tell the story from memory. Make nametags on string for the characters in the story. You will need four: Father Bear, Mother Bear, Baby Bear, and Goldilocks. You will also need three bowls, three spoons, three chairs, and three rugs or towels (for the beds) of various sizes. Choose students to be the characters in the story and have them wear the nametags. Dramatize the story while you are reading or telling the story. Do this several times with different students playing the roles.

Language Arts for Th

Thank You Notes

Materials

- scrap paper
- pencils
- stationery (lined paper with a border)
- chart paper and marker
- note to parents

Preparation: Send a note home to parents asking for a stamped envelope with the address of a special person. Duplicate the stationery for each child.

Procedure

1. Discuss the purpose of a thank you note.
2. Have the students decide on someone to whom they will send a thank you letter.
3. Write a model letter on the chart paper.

Date _____

Dear _____,

Thank you for _____

_____

_____

Thank you for thinking of me.

Love,

_____

4. Use scrap paper to write a "sloppy copy" of the letter. Help students with their notes. Encourage them to use invented spelling.
5. When the letters have been edited, distribute the stationery for the final copy. Rewrite the letters on the special stationery.
6. Fold the letters, put them into the appropriate envelopes, and mail them.

Name _____

Printing Practice for Th

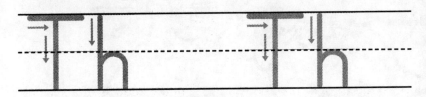

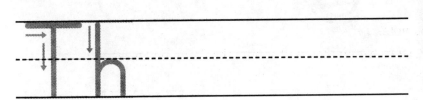

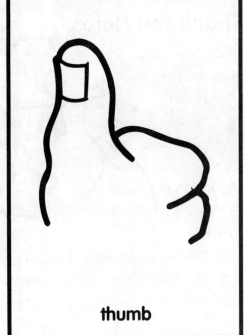

thumb

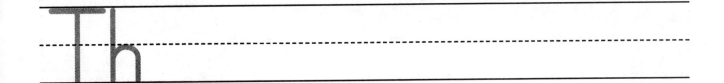

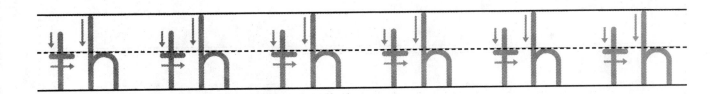

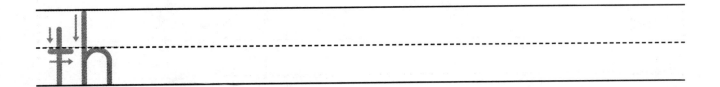

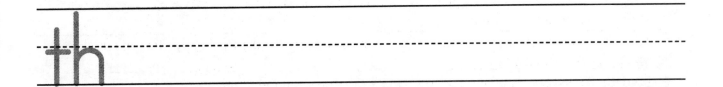

Word Practice for Th

thumb

three

thimble

I have two thumbs.

288

Science Activities for Th

Thermometers Measure Temperature

Materials

- outdoor thermometer
- calendar
- chart paper and marker

Preparation: Draw a large calendar on chart paper.

Procedure

1. Discuss the function of a thermometer.
2. Put the thermometer outside where it can be seen from indoors.
3. Check the temperature early in the morning, at noon, and later in the day. Record the temperatures in the boxes on the calendar.
4. Have a student draw a sun, clouds, rain, or snow in the box with the temperature.
5. Discuss observations and how it feels at certain temperatures.

Thunder and Lightning

Materials

- *Flash, Crash, Rumble, and Roll* by Franklyn Branley
- chart paper and marker
- sheets of gray construction paper (one per child)
- white and yellow paint
- paintbrushes

Procedure

1. Create a KWL chart. Ask the students what they already know about thunder and lightning. Write the responses on chart paper in the first column. Ask what they would like to know about thunder and lightning and put these responses in the second column.
2. Read a book to learn facts about thunder and lightning.
3. Paint white clouds on the gray paper and let them dry.
4. When the clouds are dry, use the yellow paint to add streaks of lightning to the paintings.
5. Review facts from the book.
6. Add new information to the third column, entitled "Learned."
7. Display the chart and the artwork.

Thunder and Lightning		
Know	**Want to Know**	**Learned**

Art Activities for Th

Thumbprint Animals

Materials

- paper
- stamp pads
- fine tip black markers

Procedure

1. Use the stamp pads to make thumbprints on paper, leaving space between them so details can be added.
2. With the markers, add details to make the thumbprints look like animals.
3. Display with the title, "Thumbprint Things."

Theater Time

Turn a large cardboard box into a theater and use it for puppet shows.

Materials

- *The Three Little Pigs* (any version)
- large cardboard box
- knife
- paint
- paintbrushes
- pig and wolf patterns on page 291
- 3 sheets of paper
- tape
- crayons or markers
- scissors
- sheet of white cardstock

Preparation: Duplicate the pig and wolf patterns onto cardstock. Cut the top and one side off of the box. On one paper draw yellow lines for the straw, on another draw brown lines for the sticks. Draw red lines for the bricks on the third piece of paper.

Procedure

1. Read the story, *The Three Little Pigs*.
2. Paint the three sides of the box, inside and out, with the paint.
3. Put the box on the floor with the open sides at the top and front.
4. Tape the straw, sticks, and bricks papers (each on one of the three sides) inside the box.
5. Color and cut out the pig and wolf patterns.
6. Students use the puppets to retell the story. When the wolf blows the straw and stick houses down, remove the tape and leave the sheets of paper on the floor of the theater.

Theater Time

Pig and Wolf Patterns

Duplicate one copy of this page for the class.

Songs and Fingerplays for Th

The Mitten Song

(Traditional)

Thumbs in the thumb place,
Fingers all together
This is the song
We sing in mitten weather.

When it is cold
It doesn't matter whether
Mittens are wool
Or made of finest leather.

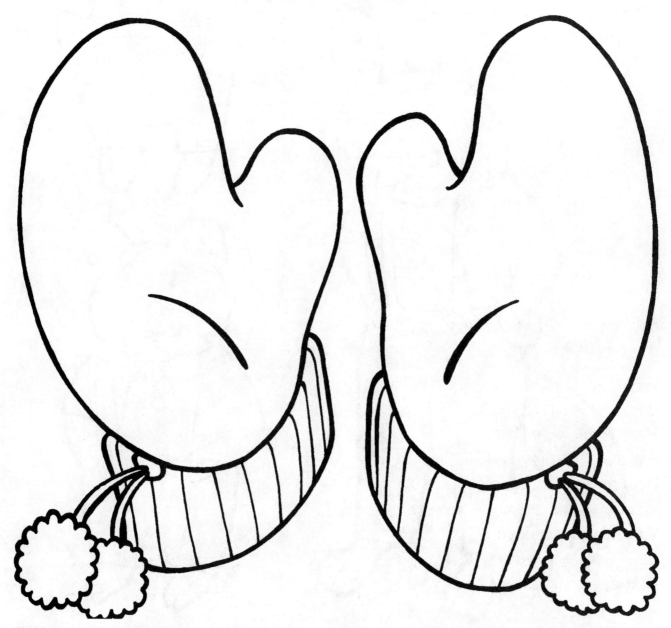

Songs and Fingerplays for Th (cont.)

Where Is Thumbkin?

(Traditional)

Where is Thumbkin, where is Thumbkin?

(Hide hand behind back.)

Here I am, here I am.

(Hold up thumb and bend.)

How are you today, sir?

(Hold up other thumb and bend.)

Very well, I thank you.

(Hold up first thumb.)

Run away, run away.

(Put hands behind back.)

Where is Pointer, where is Pointer?

(Hide hands behind back.)

Here I am, here I am

(Hold up index finger and bend.)

How are you today, sir?

(Hold up other index finger and bend.)

Very well, I thank you.

(Bend first index finger.)

Run away, run away.

(Put hands behind back.)

Where is Tall Man, where is Tall Man?

(Hold hands behind back.)

Here I am, here I am.

(Hold up middle finger and bend.)

How are you today, sir?

(Hold up other middle finger and bend.)

Very well, I thank you.

(Bend first middle finger.)

Run away, run away.

(Put hands behind back.)

Where is Ring Man, where is Ring Man?

(Hold hands behind back.)

Here I am, here I am.

(Hold up ring finger and bend.)

How are you today, sir?

(Hold up other ring finger and bend.)

Very well, I thank you.

(Bend ring finger.)

Run away, run away.

(Put hands behind back.)

Where is Baby, where is Baby?

(Hold hands behind back.)

Here I am, here I am.

(Hold up little finger and bend.)

How are you today, sir?

(Hold up other little finger and bend.)

Very well, I thank you.

(Bend first little finger.)

Run away, run away.

(Put hands behind back.)

My Pocket Book for Th

Th

thimble

1

thumb

2

She has a thimble on her thumb.

3

Wh

whale • wheel • white

Story Books

Baby Whales Drink Milk by Barbara Juster Esbensen

Big Blue Whale by Nicola Davies

Big Wheels by Anne Rockwell

The Whale by Sabrina Crewe

The Whale's Song by Dyan Sheldon

What Will the Weather Be? by Lynda DeWitt

Wheels by Anne Cobb

Where the Wild Things Are by Maurice Sendak

Whistle for Willie by Ezra Jack Keats

Foods/Snacks

- pasta wheels
- wheat bread
- wheat cereal
- wheat crackers
- whipped cream

Getting Started

1. Introduce the letter and the special picture. Read a book with the letter **Wh** in the title. Brainstorm a list of other words that begin with a **Wh** and write the words on a chart. Include the names of any children in the class whose names begin with **Wh**. (**Note:** When introducing the students to any of the activities or worksheets connected to the letter, the emphasis should be on the connection to the letter and the letter sound.)

2. Play a game of Wheel Tag outside in a safe place where you can draw on the pavement. Using sidewalk chalk, draw a very large wheel between 30' and 50' (90 m and 155 m) across with eight spokes. Choose one player to be "It." When a whistle is blown, It runs after the other players. Everyone, including It, must stay on the lines at all times. If two players run into each other, one or both can turn around, but they can't step anywhere except on the lines. When It catches a player, then that player becomes the new It.

Language Arts for Wh

Wheel of Words

Materials

- large rectangular sheet of heavy paper
- large circle, cut from heavy paper
- large paper fastener
- index cards
- tape

Preparation: Write sight words the students are learning on the index cards.

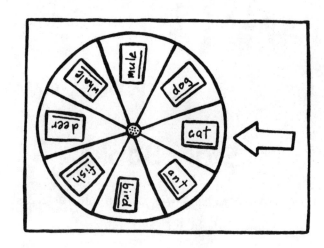

Procedure

1. Draw lines to divide the circle into eight pie shapes.
2. Put the paper fastener through the center of the circle and into the large rectangle.
3. Draw an arrow on the side of the rectangle so that it will point to one word as the wheel is turned.
4. Tape the cards to the wheel in the pie shapes.
5. Play a game. A student turns the wheel and calls on another student who then reads the word the arrow is pointing to.
6. If the word is read correctly, then that student gets to turn the wheel. If the word is not read correctly, then tell the student the word. Try to come back to the word again and give the student another opportunity to read the word correctly.

The 5 W's

Interview teachers and find out the answers to five questions reporters ask: *who, what, when, where,* and *why.*

Materials

- list of teachers to be interviewed

Procedure

1. Teach the students the five question words that reporters ask when they are interviewing people for a story: *Who, What, When, Where,* and *Why.*

2. Discuss possible interview questions that begin with the letter **W**: *When* did you decide to become a teacher? *Why* did you become a teacher? *Who* helped you become a teacher? *Where* did you go to school? *What* was your favorite subject in school?

3. Give each pair of students time to interview someone. Each pair of students will interview one teacher and report to the class.

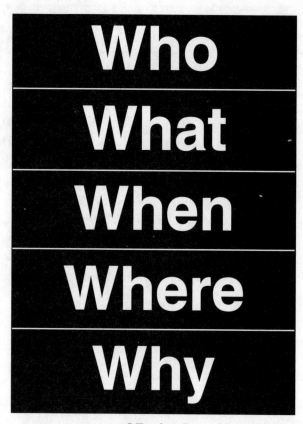

Printing Practice for Wh

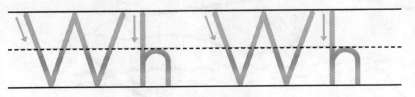

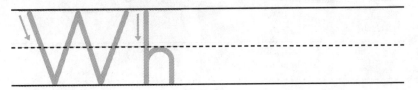

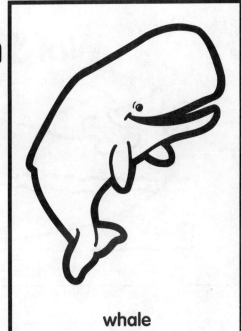

whale

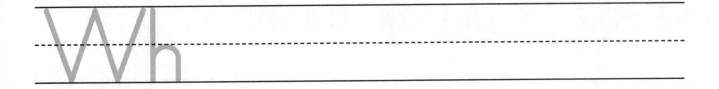

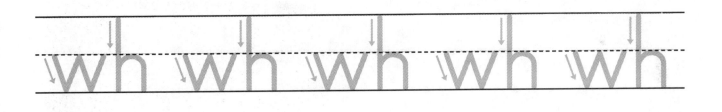

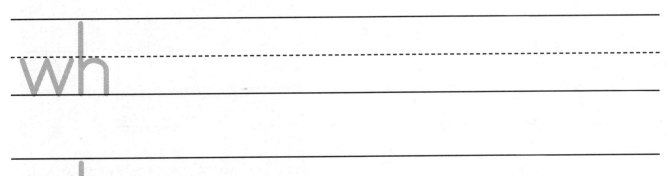

Word Practice for Wh

whale

wheel

white

The whale swims.

Science Activities for Wh

Whole Wheat Bread

Read a version of the *Little Red Hen* and find out how she finds grains of wheat and makes whole wheat bread.

Materials

- *Little Red Hen* (any version)
- bread maker
- ingredients (see Preparation section) or a whole wheat bread machine mix and water.

Preparation: Gather the ingredients listed in the recipe below.

Honey Whole Wheat Bread

1 ⅛ cups (270 mL) warm water (110 degrees F/45 degrees C)
3 tablespoons honey
⅓ teaspoon salt
1 ½ cups (335 g) whole wheat flour
1 ½ cups (335 g) bread flour
2 tablespoons (30 mL) vegetable oil
1 ½ (7 mL) teaspoons active dry yeast

Place ingredients in the bread machine in the order listed. Select the whole wheat setting and press Start. It should take approximately 3 hours.

Procedure

1. Read the book, *Little Red Hen*.
2. Make the bread in the bread maker and enjoy.

Whales

Materials

- *Big Blue Whale* by Nicola Davies, *Baby Whales Drink Milk* by Barbara Juster Esbensen, or *The Whale* by Sabrina Crewe
- chart paper and markers
- picture of a whale
- measuring tape
- index cards

Preparation: On each index card, write one of the following words: *baleen, plates, krill, blowhole, mouth, blubber, size, ears, skin, eyes, traveling,* and *humming*.

Procedure

1. Show and discuss the picture of a whale.
2. Draw a word map on the chart paper.
3. Ask the students what they already know about whales. Record their answers on the word map.
4. Ask students to remember facts about whales as you read a book about whales.
5. Read the whale vocabulary words to the students, one at a time, and have them tell what they remember about the word from the book.
6. Go to a long hall or outside. Use the measuring tape to show the size of a blue whale, 100' (30 m).
7. Display the word map and the vocabulary words with the Whale Mural (see page 300).

Art Activities for Wh

Whiskers

Materials

- sheets of construction paper (one per child)
- crayons and markers
- straw broom
- glue

Preparation: Cut straw from the broom to create "whiskers."

Procedure

1. Draw a large cat on construction paper.
2. Color the cat with crayons or markers.
3. Glue on pieces of straw for the cat's whiskers.

White Paint on Dark Paper

Materials

- *White Snow, Bright Snow* by Alvin Tresselt
- sheets of dark construction paper (one per child)
- white paint
- sponge brushes
- shallow cups

Preparation: Pour the white paint into shallow cups.

Procedure

1. Read a book about snow.
2. Use white paint and sponge brushes to paint pictures of a snow scene.

Whale Mural

Materials

- *Big Blue Whale* by Nicola Davies
- mural paper
- large sheets of heavy, white paper (one per child)
- enlarged whale pattern (page 301)
- light blue tempera paint
- blue watercolor paint
- paintbrushes
- scissors
- glue

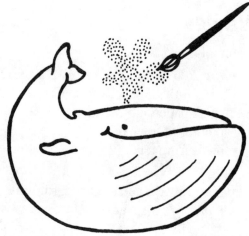

Preparation: Enlarge and duplicate the whale pattern onto heavy paper for each child.

Procedure

1. Use the blue tempera paint to paint the mural paper.
2. Use the blue watercolor paint to paint the whales.
3. When the whales are dry, cut them out, and glue them on the water on the mural.
4. Display the mural with the title, "Big Blue Whales."
5. Display the whale vocabulary cards from page 299 on the large whale outline in the appropriate places.

Whale Mural

Whale Pattern

Each student will need one copy of this page.

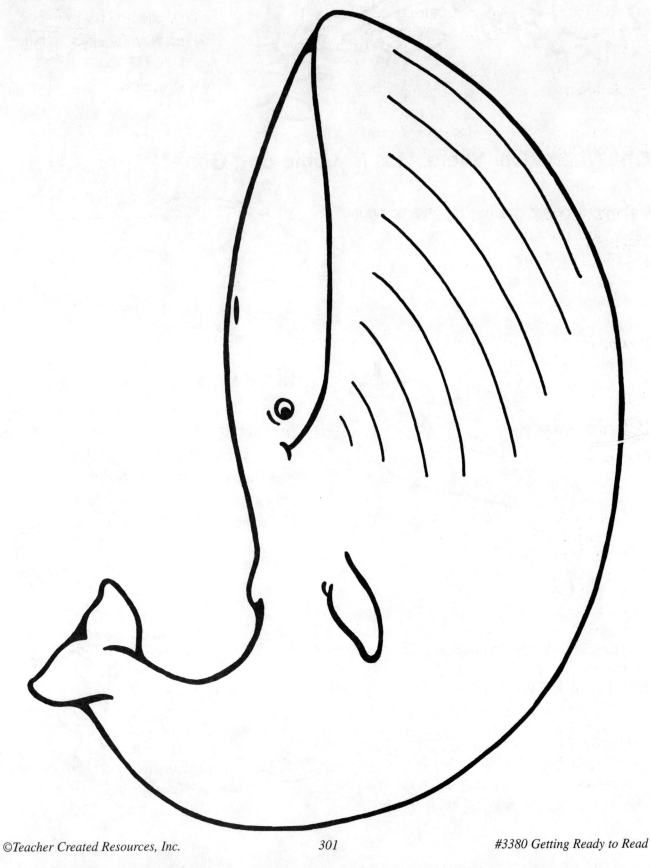

Songs and Fingerplays for Wh

Tell Me Why

(Traditional)

Tell me why the sky's so blue.
Tell me why the ivy twines.
Tell me why the sky's so blue,
And I will tell you
Just why I love you.

Oh, Where, Oh Where, Has My Little Dog Gone?

(Traditional)

Oh, where, oh, where, has my little dog gone?
Oh, where, oh, where, can he be?
With his tail cut short
And his ears so long
Oh, where, oh, where, can he be?

Big Blue Whale

(Sing to the tune of "Three Blind Mice.")

Big blue whale,
Big blue whale,
See how he swims, see how he swims.
He swims so fast he is hard to see,
He comes up for air so he can breathe,
Big blue whale,
Big blue whale.

Michael Finnegan

(Traditional)

There was an old man named Michael Finnegan
He grew whiskers on his chin-a-gin
The wind blew them off but they grew in again
Poor old Michael Finnegan, begin again . . .

Songs and Fingerplays for Wh *(cont.)*

The Wheels on the Bus

(Traditional)

The wheels on the bus go round and round,
Round and round, round and round.
The wheels on the bus go round and round,
All through the town.

The driver on the bus goes, "Step back, please,"
"Step back, please, Step back, please."
The driver on the bus goes, "Step back, please,"
All through the town.

The horn on the bus goes, beep, beep, beep,
Beep, beep, beep, beep, beep, beep,
The horn on the bus goes, beep, beep, beep,
All through the town.

The windows on the bus go up and down,
Up and down, up and down.
The windows on the bus go up and down,
All through the town.

The babies on the bus go "Wah, wah, wah,
Wah, wah, wah, wah, wah, wah."
The babies on the bus go "Wah, wah, wah."
All through the town.

The wipers on the bus go swish, swish, swish,
Swish, swish, swish, swish, swish, swish.
The wipers on the bus go swish, swish, swish,
All through the town.

The lights on the bus go blink, blink, blink
Blink, blink, blink, blink, blink, blink.
The lights on the bus go blink, blink, blink,
All through the town.

My Pocket Book for Wh

Wh

whale
1

white
2

The whale is black and white.
3